The Five Commitments of a Leader

Praise for *The Five Commitments of a Leader*

"This book does something other [leadership books]
don't: Elevates the standards for becoming a leader and
yet shows that anyone who really wants to be a leader
can become one. . . . The practice tools liberally shared
throughout the book allow the reader to apply the five
commitments instantly."

TOJO THATCHENKERY, PROFESSOR OF ORGANIZATION DEVELOPMENT,
GEORGE MASON UNIVERSITY AND AUTHOR OF *APPRECIATIVE
INTELLIGENCE: SEEING THE MIGHTY OAK IN THE ACORN*

"*The* Five Commitments of a Leader *is an inspiring,
thought-provoking and pragmatic book. The principles are
easy to apply [and] powerful in impacting one's leadership.
It's a must-read for all, since there is a leader in each of us.*"

DOLLY OBEROI, CEO, C2 TECHNOLOGIES, INC.

"A must-read for incumbent or aspiring leaders! Mark
Leheney offers his unique views on leadership along with
a synthesis of best leadership practices. . . . You will gain
great ground by following the commitment principles!"

SUSAN LANGLITZ, PH.D., PROFESSIONAL SPEAKER,
BUSINESS OWNER AND AUTHOR OF *HAVE CONFIDENCE, WILL TRAVEL*

The Five Commitments of a Leader

Mark Leheney

MANAGEMENTCONCEPTS

MANAGEMENTCONCEPTS

8230 Leesburg Pike, Suite 800
Vienna, VA 22182
(703) 790-9595
Fax: (703) 790-1371
www.managementconcepts.com

Printed in the United States of America

Library of Congress Cataloging-in-Publication Data

Leheney, Mark.
    The five commitments of a leader / Mark Leheney.
        p. cm.
    ISBN 978-1-56726-219-3
1. Leadership.   I. Title.
HD57.7.L444 2008
658.4'092—dc22

2007050969

10   9   8   7   6   5   4   3   2   1

About the Author

Mark Leheney is a Senior Consultant with Management Concepts in Vienna, Virginia. He provides facilitation, training, and coaching in the areas of leadership, management, and team and individual development. He has worked in the areas of communication, conflict, emotional intelligence, critical thinking, change, group dynamics, and personality type.

Mr. Leheney holds a master's degree in organization development and knowledge management. He is on the faculty of the Georgetown University Leadership Coaching Program.

To my family: My wife, Linda; my daughter, Emma;
and my parents, John and Barbara Leheney.

Table of Contents

Preface

There are many different ways to think about or characterize leadership—what it is, what it should be, what is right or wrong with it today, where it works, and where it fails.

These views are usually shaped by our own personal experiences, beliefs, values, culture, and other factors. You may have observed effective leadership in a particular situation and thought, "Now *that's* leadership."

However, leadership often involves ambiguity, volatility, change, and uncertainty. It plays out over the long term, and in specific moments. What looks like a failure at first may prove to be exactly what is needed in the long run. What looked good initially may prove fatal. Sometimes, it is not clear until later.

Even so, there is a way of thinking about the practice of leadership that constitutes a "lens." Holding this lens up to anyone leading—perhaps most interestingly, yourself—you gain insight into a powerful way that leadership can be assessed and understood. This way of looking at leadership integrates a wide range of what must be grasped, worked on, and then mastered for leadership to be effective across a wide range of circumstances and challenges.

That metaphorical lens through which I examine leadership is the commitments a leader makes, or doesn't, as he or she attempts to lead others. Consequently, this book explores what I believe to be the most important commitments a leader can make:

- To the self
- To people
- To the organization
- To the truth
- To leadership.

We can all look at our day-to-day and long-term patterned actions through the lens of these five critical commitments and ask a very clarifying, and sometimes tough, question: "Am I leading while staying true to these commitments?"

Leaders are certainly expected to do a great deal. Some leadership models feature dozens of specific behaviors, competencies, or techniques. Much of the impetus for this book came from wrestling with all these expectations that are placed on leaders. Through distillation, integration, and attempting to understand "What's really underneath all this?" the concept of core, essential commitments in vital areas emerged. I think of the five commitments as the source code for leadership—the fertile ground out of which effective leadership behaviors emerge.

The word *commitment* is interesting. It comes from the Latin *mittere,* meaning "to send." (Think of *transmit, remit,* or *submit.*) Your real commitments reveal what you, through your actions (not just words), send out into the world and workplace. These commitments are necessary for authentic, congruent, and powerful leadership behaviors.

I hope that thinking about your leadership commitments will help you be able to ask yourself important, accountability-creating questions, resolve to answer them in a productive way, and as a result enhance your leadership effectiveness. For once you as a leader accept that these five commitments are real, and that they matter, you are in the same stroke accepting responsibility for turning them into action.

Through self-assessments, exercises, and practice tools, this book invites you to continually ask yourself a simple question: "How am I doing with this commitment?" The accompanying CD offers resources to print and use along with the tools, techniques, exercises, and leadership vignettes provided in the book. Along the way, I hope to offer insights and help guide you on your own unique path to becoming a true leader who makes good on these critical commitments.

That can make all the difference for yourself, those you lead, and the legacy you leave.

Mark Leheney
Arlington, Virginia

Acknowledgments

I would like to acknowledge and thank:

Kathy Johnson and Casey Wilson, my managers and leaders at Management Concepts. They gave me the opportunity to write this book and remained unfailingly supportive, positive, and encouraging throughout the editing process.

The many hundreds of participants who have spoken openly and candidly—from the heart and head—in leadership development programs, classes, and coaching. Their stories form much of this book.

My colleagues at Management Concepts in the Management & Leadership business unit, whose multiple intelligences create constant learning for me.

Fellow facilitators and coaches at Management Concepts with whom I have had the good fortune to work, and who have taught me so much: Susan Langlitz, Clara Martinez, Terri Nimmons, Teresa Simons, and Wendy Swire.

The faculty at Georgetown University's Leadership Coaching Program, whose brilliance, humanity, and personal leadership were a huge influence on my thinking.

My editor, Myra Strauss, a diplomat extraordinaire, who took my words and made them read well.

A former boss, Angus Robertson, whose fundamental human decency, intellect, and modeling of leadership behavior were a huge influence on my thinking.

My former teachers, Ronald Clemons, Walter Johnson, and Larry Whisler, whose talent, uniqueness, and connection profoundly influenced my path into teaching.

The Reverends James Atwood and Edward Dawkins, two men who led against all odds.

All these people made clear, unflinching, unequivocal commitments as leaders.

And finally, my wife, Linda, and daughter, Emma, for their love, support, and daily reminders that it is all well and good to talk about leadership, learning, living, or any other concept in the abstract, but that at the end of the day, it is in everyday life that the great ideas either acquire wings or fall on the floor.

INTRODUCTION
What Is a Commitment?

"First say to yourself what you would be, and then do what you have to do."

—Epictetus

Think of an average day for you. You get up, shower, perhaps eat breakfast, go to work, open emails, take calls, go to meetings, write reports, have conversations with colleagues, and participate in many other activities that seem to consume—and usually exceed—all your available hours. Then, you probably bring work home.

We know that some of these activities matter more than others. We also know that we don't always do what is probably the most important thing to do. In your every action, conversation, and decision lies a central, inescapable truth that can open the door to a new way of thinking about leadership intention and action: *Behind everything you do is a real commitment of one kind or another.* Your actions reveal with 100 percent clarity what your real commitments are.

A simple example from everyday life helps make this clear. If you ask people what they care about most in their daily diet, the list might be topped by health, then cost, convenience, and taste. The exact order may vary, but people will usually identify the long-run implications (health and cost) as the most important.

When you shift the focus from what sounds right to what people actually eat every day, our behavior as a fast-food nation points more in the direction of a twin commitment to taste and convenience, then perhaps cost, and probably at the very bottom, health. That's why many people are overweight, suffering from diabetes, high cholesterol, and a variety of other health problems. This simple example highlights the gap between stated and actual commitments. The guilt or unease we feel when we make a commitment that does not serve us well in the long run is part of a built-in intelligence that lets us know when we are not operating in our own best interests.

At work, when you decide to take a call and be late for a meeting, you have made a de facto commitment to whoever is on the line and failed to make a commitment to the people waiting down the hall. When you check email rather than get busy on a dreaded report, you have made a commitment to the email rather than to getting the report done. When you decide not to take the risk to speak up in a meeting even though you think something is going wrong, you have made a commitment to your own personal comfort or safety and failed to make a commitment to say what needs to be said.

As in our fast-food example, when people are asked about their commitments at work, they often produce good-sounding lists that may or may not correspond to what's actually happening.

Leaders asked to talk about their commitments often lace their language with all the right-sounding words (open communication, teamwork, respect for differences, diversity), but examining the everyday workplace reality can yield a much different picture. It is easy to say we are open to feedback, inclusive, appreciative of differences in how others think, and willing to hear other points of view, but our actions can be at odds with our words.

In my conversations with hundreds of leaders in leadership development programs, courses, coaching, and assessments, a gap has become clear. Think of someone who professes a commitment to people, but who never seems to have enough time left over after the "real work" is done to help develop them. Or a leader who says he or she is committed to the truth, yet greets questions or criticisms of a prized initiative with defensiveness or hostility.

A better way to understand an organization's, or any leader's, real commitments is simply to focus on what actually happens, regardless of what is stated for public consumption or framed and displayed in the office. Understanding this distinction, the question then becomes: What are leaders—specifically, great leaders—actually committed to? One useful way to regard leadership is to distill it to five essential commitments:

- To the self—how much you work on developing yourself as a human being.

- To people—how much you really focus on connecting with those around you, in order to work effectively with them.
- To the organization—how much you are devoted to the intentions and performance of the place where you work, so that you show up with maximum energy and conviction.
- To the truth—how much you tell and invite the truth, even when it is hard, in order to keep yourself, others, and the organization on a right course.
- To leadership—how much you answer a call to lead and choose to engage in proven, effective leadership behaviors.

Through this framework, you have the opportunity to step back to reflect and ask yourself, at a basic level: Am I really committed to this? In what ways? In what ways am I not? What are my real intentions? What am I actually doing?

The word *I* is important here. When we talk about leaders or leadership, we are not only referring to people "at the top." The emerging view of leadership and leaders is that *anyone* can lead, from any place. It may seem instinctive to think about a CEO on the cover of a magazine when reading the word *leader* or *leadership,* but while reading this book keep the focus on how the commitments and messages apply not only to designated leaders, but potentially to anyone, and most interestingly, to *you.*

Think of a time when you saw someone step up and speak up when it was difficult but necessary, articulate a new and different perspective, take the initiative, help get a group organized, or otherwise demonstrate leadership in actual, real behavior. Maybe that was you. This is the new leadership model in action. It can happen anywhere. You can make it happen.

This opportunity to be a leader is linked to a change underway in organizations today that is nothing short of tectonic in nature. The shift from industrial to knowledge work means that the primary unit of production is no longer a machine, but a person. As social, self-organizing beings who have as their lifeblood communication and ideas that create value, people—particularly talented, high-performing employees—want and even insist on leadership that creates shared meaning (they care about the work), connection, and motivation. In leadership development groups the phrase that always resonates is: "Talent walks." People understand this at an intuitive and experiential level. They want great leadership.

This leadership can come from anywhere, not just the corner suite. When such leadership emerges, people are much more willing to contribute their maximum, which far exceeds "paycheck performance."

People's devotion to, and energy around, effective, self-directed work teams is an example of this.

Leaders who hold formal power in organizations are caught in the early stages of this transition from an old style of leadership, based on command and control, hierarchical structures, and simple power—"might makes right"—to a much more difficult, complex, and sometimes hard-to-grasp leadership context. Most workplaces are just not there yet, and relying on old, tired mental models of what leadership should be has led to widespread, palpable dissatisfaction.

Nevertheless, from the ancient divine right of kings to today's egalitarian and democratic structures, the shift is underway. As with any large-scale social shift in assumptions and expectations, it is messy, disruptive, difficult, and met with resistance every day—but it is underway nonetheless, and it is unstoppable. Effective leadership today bears little resemblance to what was considered legitimate or right even a few decades ago.

Another driver of this specific change is the concept of change itself. The old leadership models based on Frederick W. Taylor's notion of a factory with as few humans as possible assumed some kind of steady, predictable state. Today, our organizations are in anything but a steady, predictable state. Most are facing severe competitive threats. There is no way that organizations today can cope with the volatility and chaos they face with a static, machine-age mentality—and with leadership from only a few select individuals.

Make no mistake: The future belongs to leaders at all levels who figure out how to engage the workforce. These workplaces will ultimately win the competitive race. This is why it is an exciting time in which to exercise leadership.

How does this affect you? For you to succeed as a leader at any level, it is important to directly address your true commitments. By focusing on these commitments at a deep, fundamental level, you can grasp the big levers of change. Once you recognize and confirm your commitments, the manifesting behaviors, actions, and techniques can fall into place. For example, listening to someone deeply is easier, and really possible, only when you hold a commitment to people. Hearing what is hard to hear is enabled and fueled by a commitment to the truth.

So we begin this journey, appropriately enough, looking at you. We start by examining at some length what it actually means to be committed to one's self—the key instrument of leadership.

1 A Commitment to the Self

"It's hard to see the picture when you're in the frame."

—Unknown

"We shall not cease from exploration
And the end of all our exploring
Will be to arrive where we started
And know the place for the first time."

—T.S. Eliot

Leaders must commit to understanding themselves as human beings if they hope to grow and lead others effectively. This commitment is a fundamental starting point for everything else. While a commitment to the self may sound somewhat indulgent, it is no small, nor easy, task.

▪▪▪▪▪▪ PRINCIPLE

To be most effective as a leader, you must understand yourself as a human being.

Truly understanding the self as objectively as possible and then intentionally acting on that knowledge—those two are not the same—is a lifelong journey that inevitably involves experiences ranging from unease to discomfort to outright pain, along with bright, wonderful, gratifying moments, too. It is not a journey for the faint of heart, but self-awareness, growth, and effective, authentic leadership can be the prize.

▪▪▪▪▪▪ PRINCIPLE

Learning about and developing the self is a lifelong process, which anyone can engage in.

The great news is that it is something anyone can do. It does not require any special cognitive intelligence, gifts, or abilities. It is a capacity resident in human beings, and there are specific steps you can take to learn about yourself and grow.

As a result of taking these steps, you should come to know more about yourself, who you really are, and how you come across to others. From there, you can engage in new behaviors and even ways of thinking that maximize your own effectiveness and satisfaction.

▪▪▪ What Is a Commitment to the Self?

To start on this journey, we can ask: What is the "self"? It can be defined as the sum total of perceptions, experiences, conscious and

unconscious activity, culture, worldview, judgments, styles, preferences, values, and all components that make up you as a unique human being. The self is a complicated, unique package.

A commitment to self means understanding that you never really,
completely figure out everything about yourself. Your self-awareness
evolves and deepens over time with this commitment. This is progres-
sive inner wisdom. You can perhaps recall a time in your life when you
thought you "had it all figured out," and there wasn't much more, or
even anything else to learn. You might chuckle now at that notion.

> "By carefully analyzing every fascination (we shall) extract from
> it a portion of our own personality . . . [W]e meet ourselves time
> and again in a thousand disguises on the path of life."
>
> —Carl Jung

For example, when I was younger and studying logic I was convinced
that marshalling a logical, air-tight argument would convince others that I was right. To my consciousness at that time, right equaled
right, and how complicated was that to understand?

Later in life, after repeated frustration, it occurred to me that I had
completely overlooked the human side of the equation. This meant
things such as involving people in the thinking stage, asking their
opinions, and recognizing their ideas. The human element in influ-
encing was unconscious to me at the time. Further, my limited vision, or blindness, on this point meant that I was perplexed by resistance and push-back, especially when it didn't seem logical! Only
after more than a few instances where I didn't get what I wanted did I

start to question my own approach. When I finally realized the massive oversight on my part, big new doors opened. The self-awareness helped.

Another example many people can relate to is the dawning recognition that the work one has chosen doesn't actually bring happiness. Many people tell themselves they need to work in the field they studied for, which brings some measure of status and security, and which seems acceptable to others, particularly influential figures such as family members. Sustained introspection around career choices often surfaces emotions that have long been suppressed, particularly when the introspection occurs during the fertile mid-life period. This, too, is an example of self-awareness.

■ ■ ■ ■ ■ **SELF-ASSESSMENT**
How Has Your Self-Understanding Changed Over Time?

Part I. As adults grow and develop, their concept of self changes. At times, there may be periods of relative stagnation, followed by bursts of development. Identification with some things (people, ideas, beliefs) may shift or yield to emerging, new ones.

Using the timeline below, write down some key terms or phrases that describe your concept of self at particular stages. For example, at one age you may have held a self-concept of being steadfast, determined, or even stubborn. This may have yielded later in life to concepts such as willingness to change and open-mindedness.

Adolescence	Young adult	Mid-life	Senior years

Part II. What triggered the changes? What did you learn from these changes?

Part III. How has your understanding of self to this point impacted your leadership? Can you link the self-concept you now have with leadership effectiveness? What lessons have you learned from earlier periods in your life, when you may have led out of different styles or ways of being?

Insight	Action Taken	Results
I did way too much to please others out of a fear of their disapproval.	Heightened awareness or noticing of energy expended to make others happy. Explicit conversations around expectations and others' needs so I could choose more freely what I was willing to commit to, renegotiate terms of, or decline.	Better balance of energy and attention, clarity of expectations, and more time freed up to pursue what I think is important.

Developing a Commitment to the Self

If you accept that there is more learning and growth ahead along the road of your life, the first question is: How do you learn more about yourself? This is essential in order to then act on that knowledge to intentionally set personal growth into motion.

The following are powerful techniques:

- Understand your story
- Take the time to notice
- Use the Johari Window
- Learn your type and archetypes
- Use the Action-Reflection Loop
- Know your strengths and weaknesses
- Discover your personal mission, vision, and values.

Let's explore each of these to see how they can help you. Some will likely have more impact than others, depending on what's happened so far in your life and development, and what you sense is ahead.

Understand your story

One effective practice coaches use to help clients come to a new and often transformational understanding of themselves is helping them understand "the story." Your story, in this context, means truly comprehending—often for the first time—what you tell yourself about who you are. The story is an often unconsciously chosen narrative that explains reality to you, and often justifies your actions. It is the product of deep assumptions about the self. An erroneous, self-limiting belief is an example of a bad story.

PRINCIPLE

> Your "story" is who you tell yourself you are. As a leader, it is essential you understand as objectively as possible your story, and craft the one that works best.

Some examples of self-defining, identity-oriented stories include "I have a very busy job, a great family, no time, and a stressful boss." Or, "I am a great team member and I work well with others, but I have no life and I have questions about whether I'm doing the right thing."

Underneath these stories are deeper, nested stories that have powerful effects on how we engage the world and ourselves. "I am very competent." Or, "I have questions sometimes about my competence." A pivotal part of the story for a leader might be "You can't trust people," or "I have to do things myself." Contrast that with a story about trusting others and believing that delegation is essential, and good. The story becomes action.

The story is the product of internal scripts or "lines of code," reflecting the deep assumptions about who we are and what we are about. It is often forged early, usually in our adolescent years, and events can reinforce or challenge it. Children start to shape their story about themselves watching adults in action. Anything from a victim mentality to a sense of unlimited opportunities comes out of absorbing the messages and the narratives children see playing out around them.

The story is also the product of intrapersonal and interpersonal sensemaking. It's how we explain what is happening in and around us. The story can have elements that are very helpful and functional. That is, as a metaphorical map it accurately describes the world and the interactions we have experienced so far. Or, the story can include erroneous, incomplete, self-justifying, rationalizing, and self-deluding elements.

However accurate or productive the story, it has a powerful role in forging identity, a sense of reality and meaning, and from there, behavior, communication, and functioning in the world. You do everything for a reason—it has to make sense on some level to you. The story is the central sense-making mechanism within you.

"Everyone thinks of changing the world, but no one thinks of changing himself."

—LEO TOLSTOY

When your views of yourself and the world become dysfunctional or confused, when you consistently experience problems—particularly recurring problems—it may be time to look at your story. In other words, the focus might be turned from external events to your interpretation of those events in the context of your story.

When the story isn't working well for you as a leader anymore, when inner or outer conflict, doubt, anxiety, and self-questioning rise above a certain level, it is an invitation to ask yourself the pivotal, and often pause-inducing question posed by Dr. Neil Stroul, an executive leadership coach in the Washington, D.C., area: "Do you have your story, or *does your story have you?*"

This powerful question points to the difference between being aware of the story and being its unwitting victim.

You can often find the story in recurring problems, patterns, or systemic frustrations. Be careful, because to many people, the story conceals and protects itself through your projecting of the problem onto others. For example, when I couldn't prevail with impersonal, cold logic, the issue was others' lack of rationality. Only when I traced the problem back to how I was framing the interaction did I realize I had a bad line of code called "people don't matter" in my story.

The gift of the question about the story is that it invites leaders to consider whether they are really the sum of all their experiences, perceptions, values, opinions, and beliefs (particularly beliefs about the self), or whether there are other possibilities. Discovering that the story is often somewhat arbitrarily and unconsciously constructed, and that it is actually just one story among many, opens the door to deeper awareness of self. It means you can not only look at situations in new ways, but more fundamentally, also look at yourself in new ways. There's still much work to do on the journey, but a hugely important step has been taken. This is an enormous pivot point in adult development.

> "One key to successful leadership is continuous personal change. Personal change is a reflection of our inner growth and empowerment."
>
> —ROBERT E. QUINN

In a sense, we are victims of experience if that experience is not coupled with continuous reflection and a conscious choice of the story that is the most accurate and works best. People who are committed to the self are aware of and—as we will see—create their own story.

SELF-ASSESSMENT
Finding Your Story

Part I. Pretend you are in the middle of a movie titled *The Story of* [insert your name here]. What is the plot? What has happened and what do you know of the central figure in the drama? How would you characterize yourself in this movie? How have your decisions, actions, impressions, and history shaped the present? Where does leadership show up in the story?

Part II. Share the story with others who know you well. What do they find easy to recognize and what is a surprise to them? In what ways might you see it differently than they?

Part III. What is known in this story, and what represents assumptions, beliefs, or other subjective elements that may have been erroneous or self-limiting?

Part IV. What is the story you wish to author? What does the rest of this movie called *The Story of* … look like, with the central figure in control? What is clear, compelling, and attractive to you? Where does leadership show up in the story?

Part V. Use the table below to decide on steps that will help you create the desired story. For example:

Story	New Story	Means	Timeline
I am a hot-head in conflict.	I am great in conflict, using it as an opportunity to learn and find common ground wherever possible.	• Find and take a great conflict course. • Get coaching around conflict. • Watch people who are masterful at managing conflict and talk to them about how they process and act in those situations. • Ask people for feedback around conflict management.	One year

▦ ▦ Take the time to notice

■ ■ ■ ■ ■ ■ ■ ▦ ▦ ▦

> "The range of what we think and do is limited by what we fail
> to notice. And because we fail to notice that we fail to notice,
> there is little we can do to change; until we notice how failing to
> notice shapes our thoughts and deeds."
>
> —R.D. LAING

▦ ▦ ▦ ▦ ▦ ▦ ▦ ■ ■ ■

A simple and powerful technique you can use to understand yourself more objectively is simply to take the time to notice. Not judge,
evaluate or interpret—simply notice. This means heightening awareness of actions and reactions, internally and with other people. By
temporarily refusing to put a value judgment on what you observe,
you bypass the ego-based unconscious defenses and explanations of
behavior that often seek to justify and explain away anything potentially negative.

Simply noticing what it is happening means admitting into consciousness a larger and more accurate picture of internal and external
reality, so that you can understand more clearly what is happening.
By staying grounded in fact, you heighten your awareness of exactly
what is going on, but not, at least not yet, what it means.

■ ■ ■ ▦ ▦ ▦ **PRINCIPLE**

> Simply observing yourself, without judgment, is a gateway to
> increased self-awareness.

This practice is powerful because internal defenses kick in in a flash,
in milliseconds. An easy way to understand this is to hear that some-

one you don't like is critical of your ideas. Without even being aware of it, you probably go immediately to a consideration of all the things wrong with the other person, how unreasonable or unfair he or she is. In this way the ego keeps the kernel (or boulder!) of truth that may be present in the comments at a safe distance.

In this case, staying in the noticing stage might surface awareness of internal discomfort with the critical information, a realization you are angry at the other person, and perhaps a feeling of insecurity. By noticing and starting to understand these reactions, you create the opportunity to truly understand what is happening inside. Perhaps it is the fear of being wrong that has set everything into motion. That's quite a discovery, and potentially an opening to a new way of thinking. It might be something like "Everyone is wrong sometimes, and I can learn from the situation when that happens."

Negative emotions can often be the starting point of the journey into self-awareness. They are the doors into self-exploration, but it is not easy to be objective about negative internal experiences and the potential meaning they hold.

For another example, let's imagine someone who is perplexed by the non-responsiveness of a colleague. Despite the best and well-intentioned efforts to bring him out into the open, the colleague simply doesn't have much to say. For most people, the interpretation would be that it's all about the state of the other person, and all that's wrong with him.

Perhaps. In the noticing stage, the first person may heighten awareness of what's really happening in the interaction, without going to judgment so quickly. By standing back and noticing, for example, that he or she is doing most of the talking, interrupting, and general steering of the conversation, this person may come to realize that these signals might be causing the other's lack of response. Further, this person in the noticing stage may now perceive an undercurrent of frustration. This might be exacerbating the monologues and one-sided conversations.

By becoming aware of the whole picture in a nonjudgmental way, the first person may enable new possibilities to emerge, such as reducing his or her air time and asking more open-ended questions.

Sometimes, realizations that surface through noticing more clearly, such as "I thought I was supposed to like this and the reality is that I don't," or "I convinced myself I wasn't angry, just firm, but the fact is I was very angry," can set into motion a path of inquiry that helps a leader grow. One participant in a professional development event remarked after some exercises to increase self-awareness: "I had no idea how much trouble I was in. I was carrying a lot of anger and sadness." Whenever it might seem like committing to the self is not that important, consider this comment. Another leader said after a leadership development course, "It just hit me that I have no idea what I'm doing in my role. I've just been going along." This is a great step in self-awareness.

■ ■ ■ ■ ■   **PRACTICE TOOL**
Taking the Time to Notice

In familiar setting, such as team meeting or a regular conversation, step back from the normal functioning of just participating and begin cultivating the capacity to become an observer of the situation and yourself. Let your attention fall more clearly on what is actually happening, both in the action and within yourself.

▢ What do you see more clearly in the other person?
▢ What hunches arise around what he or she may be experiencing?
▢ What do you notice, particularly in the area of any emotions that arise?
▢ What are those emotions signaling to you?

▨ ▨ Use the Johari Window

The Johari Window, developed by Joseph Luft and Harry Ingham, is a powerful tool that can help you learn about the self. It helps configure everything from what you and those around you share as knowledge about you, to what neither knows.

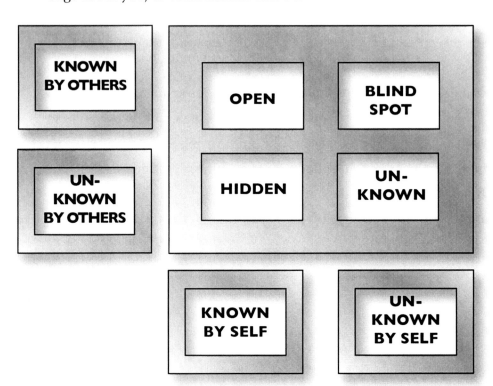

The upper left quadrant means there are things about you that both you and others understand: that you're excellent at marketing and customer contact, for example, but not so strong in budgeting and strategy, or that you have a hot button around deadlines.

The lower left quadrant means there are some things you know about yourself that you have not shared with others: for example, that you are afraid of conflict, that you are thinking of leaving for another job, or that you sometimes wish you had pursued a different career.

The lower right-hand quadrant is mysterious, and at least at the present time, unknown, both to you or others. Call it future learning that you may or may not share, or that others may realize about you at some point in the future (which they may or may not share with you).

The upper right-hand quadrant can be the most fruitful for you in learning about yourself. It represents what others know about you that you cannot see nor understand. What may be transparent to you is often very apparent to others. This quadrant is called the blind spot. As a leader, you can either make it safe for people to offer observations about this area, or you can make it so threatening that they will never get close. The most committed leaders want to know how they are perceived by others. As a leader, you can simply ask others what their perceptions are of you, your performance, your style, and your approach. This can be specific, such as how you handled yourself in a tense meeting, or more general, by asking how you come across.

▪ ▪ ▪ ▪ ▪ ▪ PRINCIPLE

Discover your "blind spots" and seek to reduce them.

As people rise through formal leadership positions, it gets harder to get honest feedback from others. Many organizations are using 360-degree assessments to help with this. In a 360 assessment, everyone chimes in on your performance—subordinates, peers, and whoever is above you. Responses to negative 360 data generally fall into two categories: denial/blame, or acceptance.

Denial and blame keep uncomfortable information away, as defense shields rise into place. Acceptance means standing back and accurately observing the messages in the data, particularly when they collide with a self-view, or the story. I once had a client blame others' withering assessments of her communication skills on the structure of the U.S. government. She hotly insisted—and with multiple interruptions—that if I truly understood the structure of the government, I would understand why others rated her so badly. In this case, the messenger was attacked, too! An important question is how often, if we are honest with ourselves, do we do this, too?

■ ■ ■ ■ ■   **EXERCISE**
Observing Others with Different Levels of
Self-Understanding

Part I. Think about someone or some people who seem to possess a high level of self-understanding. That is, they know themselves and have an authentic, real presence. What do you notice in their interactions, behavior, and communication? How do they show up as leaders?

Part II. Think about someone or some people who seem to possess a low level of self-understanding. That is, they seem to not know themselves very well and have an inauthentic, artificial presence. What do you notice in their interactions, behavior, and communication? How do they show up as leaders?

Shocks, big surprises, and puzzling disconnects between what you expect and what happens can be a prime entry point to discovering what you don't know about yourself, but others do. This is where your metaphorical map of reality breaks. Unfortunately, many people blame, rationalize, explain away, or deny the information, depriving themselves of the learning that takes place when there is a commitment to the self. It doesn't make the reality of the situation any less true; it just buries it conveniently in the unconscious mind, out of awareness and where it (only temporarily) relieves the psychological pain and pressure.

Where things are not working out, or where failures routinely materialize, can be an excellent starting point for considering what you might not yet know or understand. For example, many leaders are puzzled by a lack of motivation in the workplace. They cannot understand why people don't do exactly what they would do, with equal energy.

If a leader took time to consider the reason for the lack of motivation, this person might discover some unfortunately very common truths about his or her behavior: micromanagement, mostly negative feedback, and harsh judgments. When this information is conveyed to those responsible, the response is often defensive. "If you only knew how things were around here" is a common refrain, effectively ceding the power of choosing productive communication to the stresses and strains that are found in virtually any workplace. Clearly, this victim mentality and leadership story have serious limitations.

Another example occurs when leaders are genuinely puzzled by people who leave their organization. Such leaders are often baffled about why staff had such a sharp reaction to something they did or said. "They need to get over it," a leader will sometimes declare, not understanding that he or she is actually fostering the problem. The leader will remain trapped in this blind spot until the consequences become unbearable, or until the leader connects the dots leading back to his or her actions or words that are causing this recurring problem.

For example, I once spoke with a person who was describing a situation in a manager's department. Only after literally years of unwanted turnover was the manager finally starting to "get it," I was told.

"You cannot change what you cannot see."

—CHALMERS BROTHERS

When this happens, when you "get it," when new understanding about the self occurs, it may be experienced as an epiphany, a flash of insight, a potentially huge restructuring of consciousness. It will feel clearly and intuitively "right." It is a realization, a new awareness of what is real. It may be felt as an "Oh my gosh" moment.

In their book *Why CEOs Fail*, Dotlich and Cairo explain what happens when the opposite occurs: "Companies frequently experience serious setbacks when entire groups of people collude to overlook, deny, or manage around a CEO's negative personality characteristics. We have witnessed the demise of once great companies such as Enron, Kmart, Global Crossing, and Tyco realizing far too late that one factor in their failure was the fact that no one could tell the emperor the truth."[1]

None of this is to suggest that what happens is always a leader's fault. Workplaces are far too complex for such a simple explanation. However, a critical task of leaders is to learn as much as possible about the self and its impact on others, in order to raise the game to the highest possible level.

Learn your type and archetypes

Another powerful way to increase an understanding of the self is by exploring your own psychological type and archetypes.

Type refers to the Myers-Briggs Type Indicator®, a widely used personality indicator that can have incredible power in aiding understanding of the self and interactions with others. The theory, based on the work of Carl Jung, is deep and multifaceted, potentially launching lifelong learning.

Reduced to its simplest expression, the theory holds that some people prefer extraversion over introversion. That is, they are more energized by interaction and communication with the external world, while introverts are more comfortable in their inner mental world. Extraverted leaders tend to be more outgoing and interact more with others, whereas introverted leaders operate more behind the scenes.

The way we take in information varies, too. Sensors prefer factual, concrete, and detailed content about the here-and-now, whereas intuitives prefer processing in big-picture, thematic, and future-oriented patterns. Sensor leaders usually pay more attention to the facts and figures that are knowable, while intuitive leaders think more about conceptual plans for the future.

Once we have information, the next step is to make judgments, or decisions. Thinkers prefer a rational, logical, principled approach, whereas feelers prefer to make judgments by referencing the human values in a situation. Thinker leaders usually refer to an objective standard to make a decision, while feeler leaders tend to think more about the people involved in the decision.

The final dichotomy, judging and perceiving, refers to our outer-world orientation and lifestyle—whether we prefer as judgers to come to closure on decisions in a structured way, or as perceivers to generate more options and stay open longer to new information in a more spontaneous way. Judging leaders often seek to come to a decision and move on, while perceivers take more time to consider alternatives.

Think of meetings where some people did most of the talking and others just listened, and you may have seen the extraversion-introversion dichotomy in action. Overuse of either preference can cause problems. Extraverts can wind up doing a disproportionate share of the talking. Leaders who prefer introversion may be misunderstood because they choose to convey less to the outside world. Either one is an important awareness about how the self is showing up to others. I experienced earlier in my life situations where I sensed I had dominated the air time, and so chose to say less and create more space for others to contribute.

If you have experienced frustration over too many details and therefore "being in the weeds," or been unable to get your hands around something purely conceptual and wondered whether others were "building grand castles in the air," you may have seen sensing versus intuition in action.

If you have had trouble making a decision in a group because there was a technically "right" way to decide an issue and another way that more explicitly acknowledged the human beings in the mix, perhaps by not wanting to hurt anyone's feelings, you may have seen thinking versus feeling in operation. In organizational restructurings thinking versus feeling can come to the fore: What's the right thing for the business? versus How can we take care of people?

And when there was a disagreement on a process, or how long it should take to come to a decision, you may have experienced the tension between judging and perceiving.

No type is better than another. Although leadership positions are overwhelmingly dominated by thinkers and judgers, the key is to understand and respect both your own and others' preferences, and to become more skilled in flexing your behavior depending on the needs of the situation. It is all too easy to operate only out of your own preferences, dismissing others who have different preferences. When this behavior comes from a leader, it is particularly damaging. Culture often is a reflection of the preferences of leaders, and those who take a different approach can feel like second-class citizens.

This summary of type explains just a few basics. It is important to know that type is much more than a simple additive process with four preferences. These preferences intermingle in myriad ways. You can probably imagine how an extraverted intuitive and an introverted sensor might experience tension in communication, for example; or how a feeling perceiver and thinking judger might have trouble coming to a decision. Type ultimately reveals how we process, what is usually communicated or not, how we tend to engage the world, and what happens under stress, for example.

Carl Jung also pioneered work in the area of archetypes, which can be enlightening in the same way as type. Archetypes are transpersonal, collective, unconscious ways of seeing, interpreting, and then act-ing in the world. They surface consistently in myths and stories told across cultures.

An example of an archetype is the warrior, someone who is prone to conflict behavior. You probably also know someone who fits the lover archetype, for whom life is an opportunity to nurture, take care of, and help others. The innocent archetype manifests in someone who does not see the sometimes harsh realities of life. And the sage arche-type is all about knowing more, being wise and informed.

It has been said that three people with different archetypes can walk into the same meeting and experience it very differently. The warrior scans for who has power and must be overcome, the lover wants to know if anyone needs help, and the sage wonders what he or she can learn from the situation.

PRINCIPLE

Knowing your psychological type and archetypes can dramatically increase your self-understanding.

Some archetypes, such as warrior and ruler, show up in leadership more than others. Every individual has a constellation of archetypes that unconsciously shape his or her life, with one being dominant. Understanding what these are, how they influence behavior, and how all archetypes can be accessed when necessary is part of a journey to wholeness and integration. Carol S. Pearson has written in a compel-ling way about the power of archetypes in her book *Awakening the Heroes Within.*[2]

■ ■ ■ ■ ■   **SELF-ASSESSMENT**
Type and Archetypes

If you have not taken the Myers-Briggs Type Indicator, complete the instrument (www.capt.org), and after receiving the feedback ask:

What is your dominant function? In what ways have you used this as a leader? Where has it served you well or not well?

Where have you noticed the operation of the inferior function? What examples or stories can you recall that showcased the inferior? How has the inferior function affected your leadership?

What steps can you take to develop all the preferences, increasing your versatility?

If you have not taken the Pearson-Marr Archetype Indicator (www.capt.org), complete the instrument, and after receiving the feedback ask:

What are the dominant archetypes in your leadership? What is the impact of this on your leadership?

What archetypes do you repress, or not allow to emerge? What is the impact of this on your leadership?

These ways of understanding the self, along with other instruments, including assessments of emotional intelligence, conflict styles, and communication behavior, generally are all useful. At the same time, there is no substitute for actual experience as a way to understand the self. This leads us to the Action-Reflection Loop.

■ ■ **Use the Action-Reflection Loop**

Among the easiest-to-understand tools to foster learning about the self is the Action-Reflection Loop.

This process simply requires a deliberate, intentional period of reflection after an event—a project completion, product launch, program roll-out, difficult meeting, restructuring—anything that seems significant and potentially contains learning for the future.

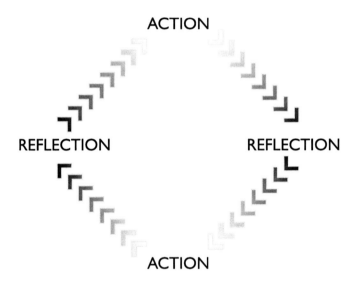

The Loop gives you a chance to look back and reflect on how things went. What went well? What didn't? What did you learn? What was missed? What was a surprise? Why? How will things be done differently next time? These questions may lead in a variety of directions, but one base effective leaders consistently touch is: "Was there any learning about myself through the experience that was important?"

Not surprisingly, heightening your powers of noticing will be a great help in this process. You might also find elements of your story, type, or archetypes in such reflection.

Know your strengths and weaknesses

Truly knowing your strengths and weaknesses can be deceptively difficult for two reasons. First, people often explain away weaknesses through rationalizing or denial. Full acceptance of a weakness can be hard. We are usually conditioned in our culture to appear invulnerable.

However, it may be even more difficult to understand your strengths. This is because strengths are often taken for granted, or assumed. For example, someone very proficient in managing a project may greet recognition of this with a statement like, "It's easy. Anybody could do it." Not quite. The fact that it is perceived as easy is a classic marker of a strength.

Weaknesses can be discerned by looking at patterns of difficulty, what seems to take a long time or a disproportionate amount of energy, or what doesn't work very well despite your best efforts.

Strengths can be revealed by not only what seems effortless to you, but also by what others notice about areas of high performance for you. Again, the patterns are the key element to pay attention to.

■ ■ ■ ■ ▪ ░ **PRINCIPLE**

Understand and act on knowledge of both your strengths and weaknesses.

With the growth of the field of positive psychology and appreciative approaches, strengths-based work is ever-increasing in popularity and usefulness. Part of committing to one's self is knowing and understanding strengths and weaknesses and making choices to leverage strengths and mitigate weaknesses.

SELF-ASSESSMENT
Strengths and Weaknesses

Part I. Draw a line down the middle of a piece of paper. In one column, write down your strengths; in the other, your weaknesses.

Part II. Consider how long it took you to record strengths and weaknesses. Was this self-knowledge immediate and apparent? Or did you have to think for some time about it? How confident are you in the assessment?

Part III. Share the information with those who know you well and whom you trust. Where do they agree or disagree with your assessment? Did you overlook any strengths? (This is common, because strengths are often taken for granted.) Did you minimize any weaknesses?

Part IV. In what areas do you suspect you may have latent capacity? That is, particular skills or competencies that you feel could expand further? What have you done to cultivate or strengthen those? What resources would help you further build those? For example:

Potential strength	Indications	Steps to strengthen
Presenter, public speaker	Good feedback on presentations	• Watch myself on tape. • Take a great course in public speaking. • Ask for assignments involving speaking or presenting.

Part V. How do your strengths and weaknesses play into your leadership role? When do you use strengths? Do weaknesses cause problems?

▪ ▪ Discover your personal mission, vision, and values

Discovery of your own personal mission, vision, and values gives power and meaning to your life, generating energy and passion.

Your mission is why you exist, your core purpose or reason for being here. It is a deeply felt need to do something that truly matters in the world. A personal mission statement might be "To heal others" or "To teach." It expresses what you need to do.

Your vision describes the results of accomplishing your mission—what happens because you lived. It's how life is different in some meaningful way because you were on the planet. It connects you to a larger outcome, or result. If the existential question is "Why am I here?" then the fulfillment of the vision provides the answer. For example, a mission of healing others leads to a broad vision of health. Teaching others leads to an educated, better-functioning society.

The key is that whatever the mission and vision for you, they seem to draw your attention. You sit up and take notice when they are not happening, and you are excited when you see them occuring. It feels right.

What are your personal mission and vision? What do you need to do, and how do you want the world to be different as a result of your having been here? You may be very clear on that, meaning that the mission and vision reside in conscious awareness, or they may be buried in the unconscious. They are there, waiting to be noticed, but they are vague and unclear at this time.

"Sooner or later something seems to call us onto a particular
path ... this is what I must do, this is what I've got to have. This is
who I am."

—JAMES HILLMAN

If your mission and vision are not clear, everything else is subject to misalignment or a lack of coherence. There is no particular direction, no beacon on which to align sight. This manifests in statements like "I don't know why I'm doing this work."

Mission and vision discovery is often described as the single most important pivot point in career management. It is easy to see how leaders must have a clear and strong sense of personal mission and vision, aligned with the organization's purposes and intentions, in order to create a compelling, authentic, and powerful connection with others who care about the same things.

"The very essence of leadership is that you have to have vision.
You can't blow an uncertain trumpet."

—THEODORE HESBURGH

Awareness of personal values is also crucial to self-understanding. Simply put, values are what you care about most deeply. They form the basis of your decisions, priorities, and actions. Strangely, the majority of participants in leadership development courses have indicated they have never consciously thought of the values most important to them.

■ ■ ■ ■ ■ ■ **PRINCIPLE**

Discover and act on your own personal mission, vision, and values.

The concept of values may seem abstract, but your values have great power in your own life. For example, seeing unfair treatment at work may remind you of a value you hold around equity or fairness. Values are often what you will fight for, so their power should not be overlooked. Instead, the quest is to understand what they truly are. A commitment to your self-identified values is a powerful force to be reckoned with.

There is a distinction here between espoused values and lived values. In the same way as we have differentiated between stated commitments and real commitments, espoused values tend to come out sounding honorable and even righteous. There's nothing wrong with that, as long as you regard those values as the high ground you aspire to. The more important piece is in discerning what values you actually hold now, and these are best detected through observing yourself and seeing what actually motivates your day-to-day actions. In particular, you can watch how you spend time, money, and attention as a reliable indicator of your real, lived values.

For example, many hard-charging executives, when asked about their values, will talk about the importance of their families, who may rarely see them.

There are many ways to engage in self-discovery, each with unique learning and benefits. Some will be more powerful and fruitful for you than others. The key is to engage. Work with the practices that directly benefit you. When you do this, you are committing to grow your self.

EXERCISE
Mission and Vision

Part I. Write down what you believe your core purpose in work to be. In doing so, how natural, real, and internal does it feel? Or is there uncertainty or hesitation?

Part II. Write down what outcomes you want to be a part of. What vision do you hold as powerful? In doing so, how natural, real, and internal does it feel? Or is there uncertainty or hesitation?

Part III. Look at your organization's mission and vision statement. What symmetry or alignment is there between that statement and your individual statements?

■ ■ ■ Making the Commitment to the Self

It may seem that after doing all the hard work described above, the commitment to the self, awareness, and growth is complete. But there is another crucial step. It is explained through the example of the very real possibility of buying a rigorous physical fitness manual and then lying comfortably on your sofa to read it.

"Awareness without action is worthless," it is sometimes said. The concept is that learning or insight not converted into behavior or other change isn't actually that valuable. An essential part of the commitment to the self is to use whatever is learned through the processes already outlined. The next step in making the commitment to the self is to understand what you can act on in order to make progress.

Below are some practices that can help you enhance your own commitment to your growth, in three basic categories:

Before you start

- Author the story
- Set specific goals based on what you've learned

Moving out

- Capitalize on strengths and minimize weaknesses
- Act on your mission, vision, and values
- Know that it may feel awkward at first
- Use affirmations
- Keep a journal

Sustaining progress

- Keep moving
- Accept a nonlinear path
- Tell others what you're doing, and get feedback
- Review at some interval
- Celebrate

Author the story

Once you know your story, the opportunity exists to deliberately change it in a way that makes life better. This means surfacing new possibilities and options for you, interpreting events clearly and accurately, and engaging work and life in a new way. Choosing to work to achieve something you want but were afraid to try is a classic example of creating a better story. Letting go of things that hold you down or restrain progress is another. As your story expands and improves, you will discover the chief limiting factor in life is yourself. There is another term for the conversion of an old or limiting story to a better one: effectiveness.

What is the story you want to author? What does it look like? How is it different from the present? What steps will bring you closer to that story? You may have glimpsed this through dreams or images when you were most relaxed and tuned in to your self.

Set specific goals based on what you've learned

Whether you have learned through the practice of noticing, the Johari Window, your type or archetypes, the Action-Reflection Loop, an assessment—or any other method—at some point you have to choose what you will do with that information. Self-discovery and growth should be in a direction you care about, not one randomly chosen. This caring provides much of the motivation.

It is best to be specific in your intentions to change. Rather than just having a vague idea that you need to work on a broadly defined area, it is more effective and practical to clearly define something to change that you can observe or measure in some way. For example, if you learned that you tend to do most of the talking in meetings, you can set a goal of taking no more than some set percentage of the air time. If you found that you tend to tell much more than ask, you can choose a simple metric of asking at least as many questions as statements made. If you found you were unconsciously tense in a negotiation, you could adopt a relaxation practice beforehand.

The problem with general intentions is they often remain that, while focused, behavior-based change is more achievable and manageable. Also, avoid the temptation to set huge, sweeping, immediate objectives—in effect, attempting to reinvent yourself overnight. It doesn't work that way. It takes time.

Capitalize on strengths and minimize weaknesses

Once you are aware of your strengths and weaknesses, resist the temptation to get too busy on the weaknesses. A substantial body of evidence now indicates that strength-based development takes you much further than trying to reduce weaknesses. According to this thinking, you cannot maximize your own greatness by reducing what's bad.

For example, if you have strengths around connecting with others, motivating them and creating a shared vision of something exciting, but are weak in budgeting or IT systems, you will not make your maximum contribution by learning more about budgeting or becoming a pseudo techie. Instead, the key is to be able to basically get by with required skills in the latter areas, and shift the focus as much as possible to where you can achieve significant results with people. This might mean reaching more people, helping them to accomplish more, and being a force in bringing people together. The message to operate out of strengths can be liberating for many people who obsess on their weaknesses.

Act on your mission, vision, and values

Paying attention to what energizes you and catches your attention is the key to uncovering your mission, vision, and values. You can also deliberately ask yourself what you want your life to have been about. Some leadership development programs ask participants to write the obituary they want to ultimately have.

An effective leader's work needs to square with his or her biggest aims for outcomes and purpose, and it can be a hard choice for someone to take a new path in that direction. The point is that leadership effectiveness is compromised when working in an area that is not truly right for you. This is the hard calculation people who have been operating inconsistently with their vision and mission must make. No one else can make this distinction for you.

"Becoming a leader is synonymous with becoming yourself. It is precisely that simple, and it is also that difficult."

—WARREN G. BENNIS

Once you understand what values you actually hold, and what values you would like to live according to, you essentially have a template to guide future actions. One step, conversation, or action at a time, you can learn whether you are acting based on the values you want to hold or based on your values in operation right now. Benjamin Franklin was famous for keeping a matrix in which he evaluated himself daily on how he was doing against what he wanted most. If there is virtually no gap between the values you are operating from and the values you most want to hold, then congratulations are in order. You have achieved a kind of congruence. For most of us, there is always room for improvement. A commitment to the self requires improvement.

Know that it may feel awkward at first

Trying anything new can feel awkward. A new conversation, action, or behavior may not feel the smoothest or most elegant. Don't go for perfect. That's a daunting standard. For example, speaking up and making a clear request of others when you previously kept mum will feel strange. Practice helps here, but don't expect it to feel as comfortable as old behaviors (such as avoiding making the request). The encouraging thing is that once you've done it, you'll feel more able to do it a little better, and a little less awkwardly, next time. An extra-verted leader may deliberately hold back a bit more, creating space for others to contribute. It will take some restraint, but it can be done!

Use affirmations

There is considerable research now behind the notion that talking about a goal in the present tense, as though it were already true, cog-nitively helps create the change you want. Nobody knows this more than high-performance athletes, who practice it religiously. Saying to yourself, "I am good at running the meeting when differences emerge," or "I am a great listener," has an uncanny way of reprogram-ming your mind to do just that.

Keep a journal

By recording what you've learned, what you did with that learning, and what the results were, you create a powerful reminder of how much progress you've made. This can be helpful when you hit the occasional dry patches, or when the going gets tougher. Also, simply writing down what has worked creates additional motivation to keep applying what you've learned.

Keep moving

Nothing succeeds like success, and momentum can be a source of strength. As you start to change what you think will be beneficial, particularly early wins will embolden you to keep going. For once you see that you can create change in the direction you want, it may very well strike you that the limiting factor all along has been you. This insight helps fuel or propel further development. For example, you may choose to engage in a new way someone with whom you have had conflict. As the other person responds positively to your insight-based change, you may be able to create a virtuous spiral, or to extend the practice to others.

Accept a nonlinear path

Staying in the game is particularly important as you encounter periods where change gets harder, or isn't working, and inevitable frustrations occur. What is being described here is not a straight, smooth line. Accept that setbacks will occur. Like most growth curves, there are periods of fertile activity, and then dormancy. That's the nature of it. Recall efforts that have paid off, and resolve to persist.

Tell others what you're doing, and get feedback

This has multiple benefits for pressing insight into action. First, by talking about it you make it more real than if it's just an idea. Second, people now expect you to do something different, so that adds to the motivation. Third, once you try something new, they can give you feedback on how it looked to them. Of course, it is best to share this information with people you trust, who are interested in your development, and who want to help. You can simply say, for example, "I realized I was making a lot of decisions without talking to others, and have been working on soliciting ideas more. Have you seen anything different in my communication?"

Review at some interval

While it is important to review your progress in real time (as in noticing), it is also a good idea to set aside time at some interval, perhaps a year or half-year or even every month, to assess the longer arc of what you're working on. It can be surprising how much change can occur over some period of time, and this practice is designed to help you fully comprehend what you've done.

Celebrate

We often rush from one thing to the next, not taking time to mark appropriately what has succeeded. A celebration of your choosing helps to solidify and consolidate your accomplishment. It also creates motivation for the next effort.

It is critical to understand that as you learn, apply, and evaluate, and then restart the cycle, the learning and growth will deepen, becoming more powerful and more fundamental in nature. You may feel like you're operating on progressively higher and higher ground, in more rarified air. That's growth, as you discover and engage the self, and it's metaphorically what T.S. Eliot is writing about in the quotation that opens this chapter. You are discovering more and more powerfully your true self, not a provisional, compromised, or fragmented version. As you do, your potential for effectiveness as a leader can rise tremendously. The significance and weight of this is important to remember as you encounter what can get in the way.

What Gets in the Way?

Even with all the promise of self-awareness and growth, there are several things that can interfere: a declaration of a static self, fear of the process, and a perceived lack of time.

The static self

Some leaders lock down on an early interpretation of who they are and resist what they may deride as navel contemplation or other introspective activities. It's not unusual to hear a leader (usually in a training or coaching session) proclaim, "I know who I am, I have been that way for a long time, and I am not going to change." This almost always signals trouble ahead as the would-be leader raises defense shields, particularly around the problems he or she is regularly encountering. The refrain is not that far from the one popularized in Washington, D.C.: "That's my story and I'm sticking to it."

In many cases, declaring a static self is actually a coping or defense mechanism against painful reminders that all is not well internally and with others. This is someone who is not open to looking at areas where problems may be occurring and sees no reason to change anything. This bias against reflection and change tends to produce rigidity, a lack of learning, and vulnerability to any events that shake up the status quo.

Today, this is a dangerous perspective. Events can change our footing in a flash, and knowing the self may be the most important attribute in navigating change. "Change or die" is the phrase, and the static self is vulnerable. Terms like "adaptiveness" and "resilience" are much more in currency today.

The static self declaration is probably explained in large part by fear of the process.

Fear of the process

This is probably the most difficult barrier, but leaders need to be strong enough to embark on this journey, wherever it leads. They are modeling the way for others. As noted in the book *Servant Leadership*, "General awareness, especially self-awareness, strengthens the servant leader. Making a commitment to foster awareness can be scary—one never knows what one may discover!"[3]

"There is no coming to consciousness without pain."

—Carl Jung

Indeed, opening oneself to important questions, surfacing long-held assumptions, and entertaining what seem to be changes to one's identity can be frightening. Questioning or challenging the story or self-concept can create inner turbulence. After all, that's the material that has brought the person to where he or she is. But from this disruption, this breaking up of sometimes very old and entrenched ways of thinking, feeling, and acting, come new and liberating possibilities within the self, which can then reconfigure the dynamic between the self and others. It is a hero's journey.

A powerful and intelligent statement of this is the thesis of the book *The Road Less Traveled,* by M. Scott Peck. The road Peck is referring to is the road of often painful self-discovery, which leads to authenticity, inner congruence, and power. The book opens with this sentence: "Life is difficult."[4] From there, Peck takes the reader on an astounding journey of what understanding the self means. It is really, simply, about growth.

The fear may also be around a perceived crucible. As Bennis and Thomas write: "We came to call the experiences that shape leaders crucibles, after the vessels medieval alchemists used in their attempts to turn base metals into gold. For the leaders we interviewed, the crucible experience was a trial and a test, a point of deep self-reflection that forced them to question who they were and what mattered to them. It required them to examine their values, question their assumptions, hone their judgment. And, invariably, they emerged from the crucible stronger and more sure of themselves and their purpose changed in some fundamental way."[5]

You are unique. What is ahead for you will be distinct. The question is whether you are willing to pay the price to achieve the self-awareness and growth that are there waiting for you. It's a choice.

As a leader, it's important to fully comprehend the positive impact of this choice. As Dotlich and Cairo explain: "When a CEO and executive committee become aware of the traits that can trip them up and learn to discuss them openly, the entire company will benefit. They make better decisions because those decisions aren't made based on unconscious impulses. They accomplish more because they're not wasting energy in unproductive and tangential discussions. Most important, they can extend acceptance to each other and build a team based on trust and accountability because they recognize and accept that all team members are flawed but valuable human beings working to manage their negative impulses."[6]

Perceived lack of time

In the ever-increasing press for action and results, many leaders squeeze out any significant time for reflection. Ironically, understanding the self better may enable the leader to spend time more productively.

The problem with not freeing up the time for this pivotal work is that all future thinking and decisions are based on the current reality and functioning of the leader. Capacity has more or less been fixed. To use a sports analogy, who would think of not allowing an athlete time to train and build before performing?

There will never be enough time for everything, but it simply is non-sensical to argue that there is no time to devote to improvement.

Lest any of this sound faddish or questionable, realize that what has been described has ancient, deep roots. This is no passing, temporary phenomenon.

Barbara Kellerman, in her book *Bad Leadership*, states: "Be reflective. Virtually every one of the great writers on leadership—Plato, Aristotle, Lao Tzu, Confucius, Buddha—emphasizes the importance of self-knowledge, self-control and good habits. But we have seen that acquiring and sustaining such virtues is hard. Intent is required, but so is time for quiet contemplation."[7]

■ ■ ■ ■ ■   SELF-ASSESSMENT
Modeling Self-Learning

In what specific ways do you model learning about yourself and thereby encourage others to do the same? For example, one leader does a 360-degree assessment every year and then publicly declares what he wants to work on in the coming year (and asks for feedback on how he is doing).

Your commitment to the self is about wisdom about who you are and want to be, and then action, in a lifelong process of learning and change. It is a great divide among people. Some refuse to acknowledge there is such a journey; others proceed with courage and boldness, learning all they can in sometimes painful moments. The payoff is growth and effectiveness as an individual and a leader.

As a leader, it is imperative that you undertake this journey. Others reliably sense when someone attempting to lead them lacks self-awareness or authenticity. The ideas and tools presented in this chapter will help you engage in this quest, as you come to more fully understand your unique presence in the world—never here before and never to be repeated—in this being called your self, out of which your own leadership can manifest.

Engage your mission and vision, face any fears, and ask yourself what change might look like. Take the time—it might just be the best time you've ever spent. From here, you will be prepared to then explore and develop your commitment to others.

ENDNOTES

1. David Dotlich and Peter Cairo, *Why CEOs Fail: The 11 Behaviors That Can Derail Your Climb to the Top and How to Manage Them* (New York: John Wiley & Sons, Inc., 2003), 146–149.

2. Carol S. Pearson, *Awakening the Heroes Within: Twelve Archetypes to Help Us Find Ourselves and Transform Our World* (New York: HarperCollins, 1991).

3. Larry Spears, ed., *Reflections on Leadership: How Robert K. Greenleaf's Theory of Servant-Leadership Influenced Today's Top Management Thinkers* (New York: John Wiley & Sons, Inc., 1995), 5.

4. M. Scott Peck, *The Road Less Traveled: A New Psychology of Love, Traditional Values and Spiritual Growth* (New York: Simon & Schuster, 1978), 15.

5. Warren Bennis and Robert Thomas, "Crucibles of Leadership," in *The Harvard Business Review on Building Personal and Organizational Resilience* (Boston: Harvard Business School Press, 2003), 43.

6. Dotlich and Cairo, 146–147.

7. Barbara Kellerman, *Bad Leadership: What It Is, How It Happens, Why It Matters* (Boston: Harvard Business School Press, 2004), 235.

RECOMMENDED READING

Beck, Don, and Christopher Cowan. *Spiral Dynamics.* Malden, MA: Blackwell Publishing, 1996.

Bolles, Richard. *What Color Is Your Parachute?* Berkeley: Ten Speed Press, 2008.

Covey, Stephen. *The Seven Habits of Highly Effective People.* New York: Simon & Schuster, 1989.

Csikszentmihalyi, Mihaly. *Flow.* New York: HarperCollins, 1990.

Fritz, Robert. *The Path of Least Resistance.* New York: Ballantine, 1989, and Creating. New York: Ballantine, 1991.

Langlitz, Susan. *Have Confidence, Will Travel.* Sevierville, TN: Insight Publishing, 2007.

Loehr, Jim, and Tony Schwartz. *The Power of Full Engagement.* New York: Simon and Schuster, 2003.

Lundin, Stephen, et al. *Fish!* New York: Hyperion, 2000.

Sheehy, Gail. *Passages.* New York: Bantam, 1974.

Tolle, Eckhart. *A New Earth.* New York: Plume, 2005.

2 A Commitment to People

"Our chief want is someone who will inspire us to be what we know we could be."

—RALPH WALDO EMERSON

Probably the single most important question to ask in an effort to understand effective leadership is: What is the nature of the relationship between leaders and others? In the content and context of that relationship lies key information on how well the organization is performing. Is the relationship strained, marked by mutual misunderstanding, a lack of trust, low motivation, and resentment? Or does the relationship contain clear communication, mutually reinforcing processes, genuine commitment, and a clear sense of moving ahead together?

■ ■ ■ ■ ■ ■ **PRINCIPLE**

> The health or quality of the relationships you have
> with others is an important indicator of your leadership
> effectiveness.

Recall someone in your work life who showed a genuine interest in and concern for you. This person wanted to know how you were doing, what your own goals were, what you liked and didn't like, and a host of other things that mattered to you—and which created a sense of connection, or loyalty to that person.

Now, contrast that with someone who showed no particular commitment. There was no indication of an interest in you, your goals, or your hopes for work. Who would you have worked harder for, and more collaboratively with? Who would you have gone to the mat for? Who would you have pulled an all-nighter on a project for?

Unfortunately, many leaders in positions of authority have significant room to improve on their commitment to people. They are committed to the goals and outcomes their organization values, they are masterful at understanding and working the technical complexities of modern organizations, but they either do not make the time to, or do not have the interest in, making a commitment to the people.

■ ■ ■ ■ ■   **EXERCISE**
Characterizing Relationships

Part I. What descriptors would you use to characterize the relationships you have with others? How do you think you are perceived? How does the relationship feel to you? Below are some adjectives. What others would you add?

Engaged   Disengaged
●——●

Supportive   Unsupportive
●——●

Helpful   Unhelpful
●——●

Interested   Uninterested
●——●

Kind   Unkind
●——●

Open   Closed
●——●

Friendly   Unfriendly
●——●

Constructive   Destructive
●——●

Collaborative   Uncollaborative
●——●

Part II. What is the impact of these relationship attributes? In what ways does each one help or hinder getting work done?

What is an organization, really, apart from its people? Certainly, an organization can succeed for some time on proprietary or patented technologies, great production processes, or other physical assets that are valuable in their own right. But rarely, if ever, will an organization enjoy such a commanding advantage through these technical or physical assets that the people who conceive, design, build, maintain, service, market, and sell them don't really matter.

A commitment to people actually means a commitment to the most powerful, generative, productive resource of an organization.

What Is a Commitment to People?

In talking about a commitment to people, we mean a global value or belief that the people matter, and that leaders help people access their best selves and make their maximum contribution.

One of the key ways to think about this commitment to people is to continually ask whether you generally operate with a focus on tasks or people—or both. Is primary regard given to the work getting done right and on time? Or is it directed toward the people performing that work (trusting that properly hired, trained, motivated, compensated, and otherwise rewarded people will achieve the desired results)? Or is it both?

While it may seem obvious that people are crucial to an organization's success and should be paid attention to, many leaders operate on the premise that "the people stuff" is a messy, hard-to-define, unfortunate aspect of organizational life. Some leaders believe that most people are easily replaceable, and that the technical aspects of the organization are what really matter.

"In organizations, real power and energy is generated through relationships. The patterns of relationships and the capacities to form them are more important than tasks, functions, roles, and positions."

—Margaret Wheatley

The fact is, both the technical and the human aspects of business matter. While there is not much of an argument in convincing anyone that the technical aspects of work are important, the conversation becomes more interesting when discussing the people side of the equation.

PRINCIPLE

A focus on tasks should be balanced with a focus on people.

If you have ever had a colleague, boss, teacher, coach, mentor, or relative who made a genuine commitment to you, to help you do things you might not have even believed you were capable of, then you know the power this kind of commitment to another person holds. You can become this person and presence for someone else, potentially for many other people.

My colleague Casey Wilson has written in depth on this topic in his book, *The Cornerstones of Engaging Leadership.*[1]

■ ■ ■ ■ ■ ■   **EXERCISE**
Others' Commitments to You

What happened when you found someone making a real commitment to you, your development, and your growth? What did you notice in your functioning, effectiveness, motivation, and energy level?

Overall functioning:

_____

_____

Effectiveness:

_____

_____

Motivation:

_____

_____

Energy level:

_____

_____

What happened when you found someone not making a commitment to you? What did you notice in your functioning, effectiveness, motivation, and energy level?

Overall functioning:

_____

_____

Effectiveness:

_____

_____

Motivation:

_____

_____

Energy level:

_____

_____

▒▒▒ Making the Commitment to People

Once you believe that people really matter in the workplace and you are willing to make the commitment to them, the question becomes: How do you make good on that commitment? Several powerful, practical, and time-tested actions you can start to implement immediately are:

- Learn to listen
- Share information
- Hold big expectations
- Understand, accept, and work with others' uniqueness
- Model the behavior and emotion you wish to see
- Recognize successes and mistakes.

▒▒ Learn to listen

Let's begin this section with the single most powerful technique I have seen in many years of working with leaders around people-oriented topics, ranging from communication to conflict to leadership. It is deceptively simple, and sometimes challenging, but it pays enormous dividends in showing commitment to people and thereby creating connection, buy-in, and support.

Here is an amazing statistic. For years, with hundreds of leadership development participants, I have asked people to raise their hands in response to two simple questions. The first question is whether they have ever worked for a great leader. Some unpredictable percentage of the group raises hands. Then I ask them to drop their hands only if that leader was a bad listener. Over years, over hundreds of people, a total of *four* hands have dropped. (Amazingly, two were in the same group.)

What does this tight correlation tell us? Certainly not that all you need to do to lead is listen. There is much more to it than that. However, it does strongly suggest that a prerequisite to great leadership is what has been called the "lost art" of listening.

True listening is a great marker of genuine interest in people—their ideas, thoughts, feelings, and perceptions. People understand at both an intellectual and emotional level that when you listen, you care. It means a lot because they now understand that their thinking *matters*. Simply put, most people want to be heard, so your listening increases their motivation.

Further, others know that you "get it" when you listen to their perspective, so they no longer have to wonder or worry about whether they have been understood. (This, in turn, allows them to be open to other perspectives, rather than endlessly repeating their point of view because they're not sure it's been heard or understood.) Your listening gives others a metaphorical "seat at the table."

■ ■ ■ ▨ ▨   PRINCIPLE

> Listening is a marker of genuine interest in people—their ideas, thoughts, feelings, and perceptions.

If this sounds at all abstract, think of a time when you were not able to get your point across to someone because he or she wasn't listening. The frustration, crossed signals, and incomplete communication are the opposite of what I am describing.

You may think, "But I listen to people all the time." You probably do, and here a distinction is necessary.

One form of pseudo-listening is being preoccupied or distracted, perhaps with the email currently on the screen. You may be thinking about all the other things on your to-do list for that day. You may hardly be able to wait to make your points, as when you mentally rehearse the statements you are going to make just as soon as the other person finishes. You may decide you actually can't wait until then, and interrupt. This is not the listening I am describing.

■ ■ ■ ■ ■ A LEADER'S COMMITMENTS

Barbara has noticed that predictable dynamics seem to have settled in her IT group. In most meetings, one or two people dominate the agenda, displaying their expertise and subtly putting down any other perspectives. As a result, some members say virtually nothing. Barbara senses they may have important ideas, but having seen people shot down, they are unwilling to speak up.

Barbara's leadership move is three-fold. First, she engages people after the meeting to ask how they see things. In listening carefully, she realizes there is actually a consensus among most participants that has not yet been shared. She individually encourages the others to express their views to the group. Second, she pledges to do the same. Finally, she engages those who have done most of the talking, and rather than accusing them of hijacking the meetings, asks what they think of participation in the room and listens to their perspective. She learns that they are actually frustrated with others for "sitting there and not saying a thing." She acknowledges the feeling and asks them what they think the reaction may have been when earlier views were met quickly with a negative response. Whatever the answer, she shares her perception that this created a chilling effect. She therefore makes a specific request that these individuals ask a question in the next meeting—"Are there any other perspectives on this issue?"—and that they refrain from an attacking posture. She may even strike an agreement where she will signal them if she notices this behavior starting.

There are no guarantees on what will be said, or what the reaction will be to that, but Barbara's leadership has created a much greater possibility that what needs to be said can be said, ultimately helping the group.

In doing this, Barbara has demonstrated a leadership commitment to the people, and to the truth—to be discussed later.

True listening means essentially emptying yourself of whatever thoughts of the day or hot-buttons are currently running and just understanding the communication as the other person means it (not just what it means to you), with the subtleties, distinctions, and feelings behind the content. This is what "getting it" means. It is not a superficial hit-and-run. It is deep, committed listening.

It need not run for hours. Many aspiring leaders worry that others will take far too much time, given the opening. The time and topics appropriate for this kind of listening are those designated for discussion and negotiation. (You might set aside a particular block of time, for example.) It is not an open-ended invitation to talk about anything and everything forever, but rather a communication behavior you can use when something truly important is in the air. When it's urgent or an emergency, you may need to be much more directive. That's the time to execute or perform, perhaps by direct telling. However, when the time is available and the subject really matters, this listening skill is very powerful in engaging and helping others.

■ ■ ■ ■ ■ **PRACTICE TOOL**
Active Listening

Active listening means to listen fully, undistracted by internal dialogues or your own meanings connected to what others say. It means listening to understand what they are saying means to *them*. It calls for suspending opinions, observing carefully the words and body language, and the entire message being transmitted. Active listening is not for every conversation, such as when something needs to be done immediately. However, when the speaker is surfacing something truly meaningful or significant, it can be a cue to listen fully.

In the next few conversations of this type, practice the habit of not speaking up, not interrupting, and not injecting your own interpretation into the dialogue. Instead, just listen. Relax and focus into the conversation. Realize that this will take practice. You will experience distractions.

Over time, what do you notice happening inside you as you scale back your comments and stay longer in listening? What do you learn from others that you suspect might not have been learned with less committed listening? How do others say they feel about being listened to? Be sure to ask this last question intentionally—truly being listened to is often described as a huge motivator for people in the workplace.

When you adopt a stance of powerful listening, people often clarify their own problems and solutions (and sometimes give you the credit for solving the problem, even when you said nothing!), and you gain great information on what is happening. With this, your comments and suggestions are much more likely to be on target.

Leaders who are routinely dismissive of, or impatient with, others' ideas, particularly when they are in conflict, send strong signals about the degree to which they are committed to people. Listening is a big marker of the commitment.

Share information

One of the best things you can do to show commitment to others is to share information as widely and freely as possible. This matters for several reasons. First, people rightly feel they have better information on which to base better decisions. Second, they feel that they have more power, since information is just that. Third, it is frustrating for people to do work without knowing why they are doing it. Understanding the context of an activity is critical for motivation.

■ ■ ■ ■ ■ **PRACTICE TOOL**
Sharing Information

Think through what information you have or have access to on some regular basis that might be valuable to others. Choose a method that makes sense to you for conveying that information—meeting, conference call, email, etc. Let others know you are trying to increase information sharing in order to help them. After several occurrences of this information sharing, ask others what their perception of the practice is.

Do they find it helpful?

How does it help them?

Is it worth their time?

What else do they want to know?

Particularly for managers and leaders with formal power and information coming from above, the mantra is "relentlessly share context." This means to continually keep others in the picture regarding what the organization is experiencing. It makes everyone smarter.

■ ■ ■ ■ ■ ■ **PRINCIPLE**

The more information you share with others, the better the quality of their decision-making.

The opposite can clarify: If you have ever worked away at a project and discovered too late a missing piece of information that would have changed your approach, you know why this matters. "Nobody told me that!" is a refrain heard too often in organizations.

Leaders who routinely hold information close to the chest sometimes think they are protecting others from any unpleasant realities, but people usually have a sixth sense for such things and come to lose trust when they sense that information is being withheld. Clearly, the sharing of information, particularly when it's hard, also relates to the commitments to the truth and the organization.

Hold big expectations

Effective leaders have big expectations for others. They convey that they believe the individual is capable of great things, and their actions reflect this belief. In essence, they hold a larger vision of the other person than he or she may be holding. Think of the Pygmalion Effect. Dale Carnegie's imperative "Give the other person a fine reputation to live up to" is representative of this.

PRINCIPLE

> Your expectations of others have a powerful effect on performance.

Knowing that someone believes you can accomplish significant things provides a powerful source of motivation. Today, when many workplaces experience the negativity that can result from stress and problems, this core belief can keep people in the game, persisting and giving their best effort to make the expectation a reality. Simple statements such as "I believe you can do this" may be all it takes. Talking about a stretch goal is another way. Of course, the belief and expectation have to be genuine.

PRACTICE TOOL
Holding Big Expectations

How big is the picture you currently hold of others? How far can they go? What could they accomplish?

Share your expectations with others. What reactions do they have?

Discuss with them how they could achieve their goals. How can you support them in this effort? What happens when they see you supporting them in this way?

Understand, accept, and work with others' uniqueness

Part of committing to others is accepting and embracing their uniqueness. Much of the research on talent and high performance indicates that the key to success is understanding what each person uniquely can do.

In his book *The One Thing You Need to Know*, Marcus Buckingham argues that people are unique, and they need to find what they do best. Leaders understand and facilitate this process, rather than create a climate or culture designed to replicate themselves.[2]

"Never hire or promote in your own image. It is foolish to replicate your strength and idiotic to replicate your weakness. It is essential to employ, trust, and reward those whose perspective, ability, and judgment are radically different from yours. It is also rare, for it requires uncommon humility, tolerance, and wisdom."

—DEE W. HOCK

Buckingham and coauthor Curt Coffman write in another book, *First, Break All the Rules,* "This radical approach (focusing on a person's strengths instead of weaknesses) is fueled by one simple insight: Each person is different. Each person has a unique set of talents, a unique pattern of behaviors, of passions, of yearnings. Each person's pattern of talents is enduring, resistant to change. Each person, therefore, has a unique destiny."[3]

PRINCIPLE

Leading others means accepting they are not just like you. They are unique.

Stephen Covey, in his book *The 8th Habit,* says individual greatness resides in the intersection of passion, talent, need, and conscience.[4] You may discover these things about others through deep listening. The notion is that there is something each person can do that is distinctive and great in its own way. Leaders committed to people understand and seek that something. They value individuality and uniqueness, rather than suffer discomfort that everyone in the organization isn't just like them. Particularly with very strong-willed leaders, others often unconsciously take on their physical and communication mannerisms, in everything from vocabulary to body language. In the process, they become bad copies—inauthentic clones.

The uniqueness may seem unconventional to you, but great power shows up here, and accepting the individuality can help unlock it. You may have experienced a workplace where you felt that you couldn't be yourself, versus a place where you were encouraged to be just who you are. It's a big difference.

Model the behavior and emotion you wish to see

Leaders should model the key behaviors they wish to see in others. They should be open, ask questions, be vulnerable, be honest, tell the truth, and ask for feedback. This will not only help those around them feel safe, but it also will create a culture conducive to great leadership and organizational performance. The relationships leaders have with people make up much of their real power and influence. Leaders have to understand the impact they have on others.

The word *resonance* is important here. It is related in its origin to the word *echo.* If you want a kind of echo of intention and harmonic action—action that is aligned and mutually reinforcing—then it is worth considering what kind of resonance you are creating. What happens when you show up? What is the mood, or emotion?

Resonance can work either negatively or positively. Leaders can "trigger" or invoke either state in most people they are leading, simply by the way they communicate and act.

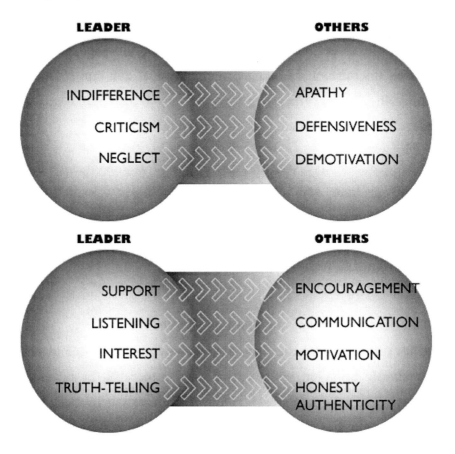

An old story illustrates: A person moving into a new town asked a villager what the people were like there. The villager asked, "What were they like where you came from?" The newcomer said, "Wonderful." The villager said, "I think you'll find them that way here, too." Later, another person arriving in town asked the same question. When he disclosed that the people in his home town were mean-spirited and petty, the villager said, "I think you'll find them that way here, too."

■ ■ ■ ■ **PRACTICE TOOL**
Modeling Behavior and Emotion You Wish To See

How do people normally act around you? What states do they typically fall into? Happy? Tense? Open? Reserved?

Choose a state you think would improve communication and working, and then model that behavior at appropriate moments, consistently. Over time, what changes do you notice in others?

The point is clear: Leaders can create conditions in which others either find their best selves and contribute their maximum—or not. Of course, what you do relates to the work explained in chapter one on making a commitment to yourself.

Recognize successes and mistakes

Even when it's busy, it's important to take the time to clearly recognize others' successes. There are many ways to do this, and what you do should hinge on what is most effective with the other person. Some like public recognition; others find it embarrassing and would prefer a private word. A symbolic, even humorous artifact such as a poster or trinket can be powerful—you will often find people placing these in prominent places in their workplace. What gets really noticed by many is when someone in a high-level position does the recognizing.

■ ■ ■ ■ ■ ■ **PRINCIPLE**
Recognize others' successes and mistakes.

Whatever the setting, the key is to be specific about what was done. General, vague statements like "Great job!" don't actually give the other person much actionable information. Better is: "That was the best presentation I've seen in a long time. The tight organization and those great quotations really helped me understand the issue." A genuine compliment can motivate a person for a very long time.

■■■■■ **PRACTICE TOOL**
Recognize Successes

Pay increased attention to others' accomplishments and select a way to recognize them. Some possibilities include face-to-face compliments, email, or recognition in a group setting. Be sure to be specific about the accomplishment. What do you notice in others' reactions and motivation as you highlight their successes? How do they respond? How does it appear to affect their work?

One of the worst mistakes you can make is to do nothing when someone has succeeded. This lack of recognition is initially puzzling, then often taken as "No matter how hard I work or what I accomplish, this person will never be happy." Failing to recognize (and, where appropriate, reward) successes is guaranteed to discourage and diminish motivation.

Of course, the opposite can happen. Performance didn't happen, or some other kind of mistake was made. People can benefit from learning about and from their mistakes, and leaders can help them do so. Instead of berating or unproductively criticizing them, leaders with a commitment to people address the problem in a way that helps the other person do better next time. This is about being constructive and positive toward a new outcome. It is easy to make it feel dangerous to engage in this discussion, and the challenge is to help the other person feel supported through the process.

You can do this by simply saying, "I'd like to help," and again, it must be genuine. The Learning Loop discussed in chapter one can help you and the other person to reflect on lessons learned and actions for next time.

All these actions will help you demonstrate your commitment to others, but it is also important to be prepared for what might get in the way.

■ ■ ■ ■ ■   **PRACTICE TOOL**
Working With People

Write down the things you find most challenging, stressful, or difficult in working with people generally. As you reflect on this discomfort, what, if anything, could it be telling you about how you frame the issue—how you look at it? What is another way to look at the difficulty you experience? Have you intentionally or unintentionally played a role in co-creating the challenges? What might others' perspectives be on working with you?

For example, a source of stress might be different personality styles in some of your direct reports. Typically, these can include anything from Myers-Briggs Type preferences to how time is managed, or how meetings are conducted. An example below works through a hypothetical progression. The key is to be able to see your issue through others' eyes.

Your source of stress, challenge, or discomfort	Other perspectives on the issue	Your possible role in co-creating that source	A new framework for re-addressing the source
People take "too long" to get to the point.	We're constantly hurried to "bottom-line" everything, and rarely explore what's really going on, underneath the superficial level, with anything. As a result, we make mistakes in diagnostics and execution.	Conscious or unconscious fears that discussions will meander off topic and waste time, leading you to hurry up communication.	Intentionally choose times to let the conversation happen, and identify times when it's important to move quickly to conclusions—i.e., emergencies or urgent situations. Clarifying the two will help everyone understand shared "rules of the game" and know how to show up in a situational context.

Are there specific people you find it more difficult to make a commitment to? What is happening in that relationship that makes it difficult? For example, if you have difficulty with Sam, what is involved? An example of new action coming out of reflection is given below.

Person	Behavior	Impact	Reflection	Action	Result
Sam	Withholding	Uncertainty, not knowing where Sam stands	What is it in Sam that prompts or explains withholding? What specific actions could I take to help him communicate more?	Share more information with Sam. Ask open-ended questions.	Sam reciprocates, opens up more.

What Gets in the Way?

By now, the case for making the commitment to people should be clear, and a handful of powerful steps to make that commitment real should be understood. If it's so straightforward, though, why wouldn't everyone already be doing these things? To answer this, we explore several important factors:

- Not genuinely enjoying working with others
- Task dominance
- Disdain for the people side
- Not walking the talk
- Leaders who know everything
- Thinking differences are bad.

Not genuinely enjoying working with others

A critical threshold for anyone wanting to lead at any level is the question: "Do you genuinely enjoy working with people?" You may have heard the infamous story about an employee who applied for a job at an organization and wrote in his cover letter: "It is best that I not work in any position involving contact with human beings." At least he deserved credit for honesty. He simply wanted to code software off in a corner somewhere, undistracted by people issues.

Some participants in leadership development courses have talked about taking a management or formal leadership position as akin to virtually hand-holding or listening to endless complaints. This negative feeling can reflect an aversion to engaging the people side of an organization, and it misses the potential and opportunity present in any work with other human beings.

Once, I was touring a large database facility with my manager, where a technician explained the incredible nature of the plant, with redundant systems, network intelligence, and real-time diagnostics. I marveled at the servers and systems, to which our host replied, "It's not that much really. It all makes sense when you break it down. I could never do what you guys do."

"What do you mean?" we asked?

"Work with people," he replied.

Engaging this barrier means asking yourself, honestly, how much working with people is part of the picture you want. It has been said that we don't lead machines, buildings, or land. We lead *people*.

■ ■ ■ ■ ■ ■ ■ ■ ■ ■

"I suppose leadership at one time meant muscles. Today it means getting along with people."

—INDIRA GANDHI

■ ■ ■ ■ ■ ■ ■ ■ ■ ■

Task dominance

As mentioned earlier, resistance to making a commitment to people often is revealed when task-dominant leaders insist that job number one is to get the work done, not to discuss people issues. They claim that they come to work to accomplish something real and practical.

Poor leadership behaviors often occur under the never-ending crush of getting work done, with deadlines looming, problems emerging, and threats materializing. By focusing exclusively on solving the problem at hand, ineffective leaders fail to distinguish between the short run and the long run.

> ■ ■ ■ ■ ■   **PRACTICE TOOL**
> Making the Time
>
> Keep a log for one week of times when you do something that you believe shows
> a commitment to people and their development—for example, asking them what
> they are learning in their work or what their own goals are.
>
> Next, design an experiment in setting aside time in your calendar for the express
> purpose of working with people to increase their effectiveness—it could be
> coaching, mentoring, checking in on how they are doing, or helping them
> learn a new skill. Schedule this time as you would any meeting—make it a real
> commitment. How much time do you think is manageable, given all the other
> time pressures at work? How can you best use that time? There are 2,400 minutes
> in the 40-hour workweek. How many do you think you should or could devote to
> these kinds of conversations?

Yes, the work gets done and the crisis passes, but others are often
unhappy at how they have been treated or communicated with. The
conditions have been put into place to degrade individual, and therefore organizational, results. The die is cast.

When a leader's sole measure of success is "We get the work done,"
without regard for interpersonal and communication skills, he or she
effectively shuts down the capacity to learn—and to lead.

There *is* a time to focus on the technical work. There *is* a time to
focus on people. This distinction and awareness of it are critical to
keeping an engaged workplace—one that will far outperform one
where people do the minimum to keep getting paid.

One example of task dominance squeezing out a people orientation
is found in the nearly universal example of someone highly competent in a technical function taking on responsibility for supervis-
ing, managing, or leading others. This often comes in the form of

taking a team-lead position. You have probably seen cases where a star technical performer practically self-destructed in a more visible, people-oriented role. There are some recurring themes here: the person wanting to go back to just doing the technical work, resenting the meetings, ignoring or being bewildered by issues such as how to manage conflict in the team, and feeling that he or she used to be good at something and now is wasting time.

Some leaders may rationalize the lack of focus on and engagement with people as a regrettable, but necessary, result of a very busy, task-focused culture. But this attitude affects two issues that virtually all leaders would agree are central: employee motivation and loyalty. Many leaders who treat people as merely work objects seem to be genuinely baffled when others resist putting forth effort and demonstrating loyalty.

As a discipline, business process reengineering failed largely because it took a mechanistic view of people. You may have heard the story about a project manager who spent months locked in his office, designing the "perfect" project plan with tidy graphs and workflows and carefully defining all responsibilities and sub-tasks. He was stunned when people resisted and did not perform in accordance with his project plan. He had no clue that they would have liked to have been consulted in advance about the goals and means to accomplish the work.

■ ■ ■ ■ ■ ■ ■ ■ ■ ■

"One measure of leadership is the caliber of people who choose to follow you."

—DENNIS A. PEER

One fairly recent development in the area of the commitment to people has been the entrance of Generation Y into the workplace. Shown no particular commitment by others, they are quick to leap, looking for someone who takes an interest in their development. This is a generation adept at change; they bring no particular loyalty to a workplace until some is shown to them. Then the game changes.

Disdain for the people side

Much more troubling are leaders who not only don't want to make the commitment to people, but also regard it with something resembling derision. Leadership development with an emphasis on people development was characterized as "charm school" once by a colleague (who was later demoted because of his lack of people skills). Frankly, there is little anyone holding this view can do to make good on the commitment. The fact is, such a person is not ready.

For some, however, a wake-up call can come in the form of a crisis, apparently unsolvable problem, or harsh feedback. This is a key person quitting, a customer complaining, protracted lack of cooperation from others, or even a spouse commenting on behavior and personality. Whatever the source, some leaders are fortunate enough to hear it in time to reconsider some of their most fundamental assumptions about the role of people in the workplace. Others remain legendary for having destroyed morale and any sense of connection. This is a sad, complex issue, and there are many components to it. The point for now is that wanton disregard for the people side of an organization equals ineffective leadership. Again, only you can determine where you are on this issue.

■ ■ ■ ■ ■ **PRACTICE TOOL**
Talk to the Best

Interview people who are known to be very good with people. Share with them your perception of their skill in this area, and ask the following questions:

What experiences have shaped how you approach people?

What do you think about when communicating with others?

What lessons have you learned?

Where do you see others who are not so skilled falling short?

What specific behaviors do you find most helpful in communicating with others?

Not walking the talk

It may seem offensive to suggest that to many leaders people don't matter much. But think about it: How many organizations have you been in where you felt people weren't really valued, as evidenced by the actions of the leaders? What stories have you heard friends and colleagues tell about how their leaders interacted with people? There is a big, and uncomfortable, gap between what some leaders say for public consumption ("people are our most valuable asset"), and what they actually do, particularly under the pressure of increasing demands.

The view that people are expendable can severely affect the organization's bottom line. Organizations incur huge, usually off-the-balance-sheet financial costs in turnover and lost knowledge. The impact on morale and productivity is harder to calculate, but also significant.

Leaders who know everything

The "people are expendable" view is often associated with leaders who consider themselves the smartest people in the room. Confronted with such arrogance, others rarely bother to do much thinking or problem-solving themselves. No questions, no discussion, no learning.

A side effect of this perception is that such a leader can often feel the weight of the world on his or her own shoulders. Jim Collins captures the essence of this leadership view in his book *Good to Great,* when he discusses the model of the "genius with a thousand helpers."[5] Leadership can be a difficult job under the best of circumstances, let alone when others don't know what they need to know to help in meaningful ways. These leaders may leave work late at night with hundred-pound weights on each shoulder.

Thinking differences are bad

Another dimension in which leaders can experience problems is gaining a clear-eyed view of the workforce. Leaders may unknowingly assume that everyone should be more like them—their outlook, style, thinking, worldview, and way of operating. You may have seen cultures where people began emulating the mannerisms of leaders. As explained earlier, it is actually out of their own uniqueness that others' greatness can emerge. Being a clone is no path to maximum contribution, but rather a compromised existence.

EXERCISE
A Work Weekend

Imagine this scenario: A project comes up for you that requires others to drop everything and work straight through a weekend. As you ask for their help, what do you think the reaction will be? (Note that leaders who have shown a commitment to people will generally have many people who will immediately ask "Where do we start?" and will show up with enthusiasm, eager to help. Leaders who have not made the commitment can expect resistance, excuses, and anger.)

There was a time when a commitment to people could be a distant second to a commitment to the tasks of an organization. Machines produced the goods, and people were easily replaced. That age is largely gone, but mental models can lag reality.

Today, high-performance workplaces and leaders in the knowledge economy understand clearly that people supported, helped, and engaged are the key to success. In such environments, people show up enthusiastic, ready to give their best and better able to work with others to tackle the inevitable problems and challenges any workplace has.

The successful workplaces of the present and future have leaders who have made the commitment to people. Have you made the commitment?

ENDNOTES

1. Casey Wilson, *The Cornerstones of Engaging Leadership* (Vienna, VA: Management Concepts, 2008).

2. Marcus Buckingham, *The One Thing You Need To Know ... About Great Managing, Great Leading and Sustained Individual Success* (New York: Simon and Schuster, 2005).

3. Marcus Buckingham and Curt Coffman, *First, Break All the Rules: What the World's Greatest Managers Do Differently* (New York: Simon & Schuster, 1999), 141.

4. Stephen Covey, *The 8th Habit: From Effectiveness to Greatness* (New York, Free Press, 2004).

5. Jim Collins, *Good to Great: Why Some Companies Make the Leap ... and Others Don't* (New York: HarperBusiness, 2001), 45.

RECOMMENDED READING

Carnegie, Dale. *How to Win Friends and Influence People.* New York: Simon and Schuster, 1981.

Katzenbach, Jon, and Douglas Smith. *The Wisdom of Teams.* Boston: Harvard Business School Press, 1993.

Rock, David. *Quiet Leadership.* New York: HarperCollins, 2006.

3 A Commitment to the Organization

"Give people a convincing reason and they will lay down their very lives."

—Patrick Dixon

With commitments to the self and others defined, we now turn our attention to what it means to be committed to the organization. After all, the organization is where everything comes together in the form of real work toward real ends getting accomplished.

Here, we ask: What does it mean to be committed to the organization? How does that happen? What does it look like? What can get in the way?

In answering, we look at the roles of mission and vision, and how values influence those. Further, we explore how these commitments can be converted into action—behavior that demonstrates the commitments and marks you as a leader. We also address how a clear-eyed, truth-anchored assessment of the organization constitutes the commitment.

What Is a Commitment to the Organization?

Let's begin with why the organization exists in the first place.

Mission

The mission of an organization can be thought of as, quite simply, why it exists. It's the overarching purpose of the organization, the rationale for its operating. Mission statements are written from the standpoint of what the organization does, in the broadest sense.

Whether it ever gets written down or not, there is a mission for any organization. There is always some implicit or explicit reason for any group of people to come together to accomplish something.

The mission statement should be clear and direct. If you can't boil it down to succinct, powerful statements, you may be hedging, or unclear. It's usually a sign of trouble when people aren't exactly sure what the mission of their organization is.

Some examples of mission statements include:

- Help returning veterans reestablish their lives
- Educate others
- Help the unemployed find jobs
- Protect the public
- Improve the quality of life for single parents.

Notice how each of these presents a crystal-clear sense of the *raison d'etre* of the organization. There is a simplicity and straightforwardness that is vital for the mission to be felt as real.

It is crucial for leaders to have a sense of taking responsibility for helping organize and guide the efforts of others toward the mission. Yet, they can't force anyone to accept or buy into the organization's mission. Effective leaders can only invite others to be part of this shared meaning. It is a matter of willing and eager commitment, not forced compliance. The more leaders involve others in understanding and appreciating the mission, the more support and commitment there will be.

Here is an example from everyday life that makes the power of mission clear: How can you motivate someone to spend time on a project that pays nothing, is performed in a crowded, badly lit basement, and involves no more than stuffing and licking envelopes, or other menial tasks?

You do it by engaging others when this work is part of any community or social cause you strongly support. In this case, your work is an integral part of a larger outcome you value deeply. Simply stated, it's worth it.

This is why the role of connecting work to mission is crucial. When the mission is real, when it calls to the person and involves him or her in something larger, it inspires dedication and focus.

Henry Mintzberg, writing in the *Harvard Business Review*, says, "Leaders engage others by, above all, engaging themselves. They commit to their industry, their company, their jobs—seriously, quietly. Instead of preparing to spring to better ones, they stick around to live the consequences of their actions. That is how they earn the respect of those they lead, and so engage them."[1]

Leaders are committed to the mission—they believe in it, want to be a part of it, and find it to be a natural extension of what they care about in life. Do you believe in the mission? Is it compelling enough for you to make the commitment?

Vision

If the mission is the purpose of the organization, then the vision represents the image of a desired future. The vision is what exists as a result of the mission having been exercised. The vision describes how life is different in some meaningful way for some group of people as a result of the organization having existed.

Note that visions are both short- and long-run. When successful work results in the vision coming true, another, higher-order vision takes its place. The vision can evolve.

The organizational vision may include achievements such as good health, security, safety, communication, comfort, choice, creativity, freedom, education, entertainment, or mobility.

In the examples cited above related to mission, a mission of helping returning veterans reestablish their lives would have a vision of settled, productive, healthy, and happy veterans. A mission to educate would lead to a vision of an educated public. A mission to help the unemployed find work would have as a vision full employment.

■ ■ ■ ■ ■ **PRINCIPLE**

> The mission statement captures why the organization
> exists—its core purpose. The vision expresses the results the
> organization wishes to bring into existence.

Inside the visitors' entrance at the U.S. Department of Labor, there used to hang a large poster displaying a stark black-and-white photo of a girl, perhaps around ten years old, at the turn of the last century. Her face was grimy, her clothes tattered, and she looked sad and forlorn. She was standing next to a huge machine in an industrial plant.

We don't see scenes like this much in this country anymore. The photo served as a reminder to everyone who walked by of an important part of the department's vision, as articulated in child labor laws; in essence: Kids should be learning in schools, not working in factories. We help make that a reality.

Leadership committed to a real, compelling vision tends to operate in an authentic, powerful way. In contrast, a vision focused only on making money is bankrupt, particularly when the leadership talks about a good-sounding vision but operates only according to the financials. It's very hard to get employees psychologically invested in and motivated by the concept of making someone else rich. They want their work their entire lives to have mattered in a different way.

Just as with mission, the vision provides the power, energy, and motivation for the organization to do the hard, disciplined work necessary for the vision to become a reality. It provides meaning. It evolves into leaving something behind as a legacy.

If the organizational vision is not clear, everything else is subject to misalignment or a lack of coherence. There is no particular direction, no beacon on which to align sight. This manifests in statements like: "I don't know why I'm doing this work." Or, "We don't know what business we're in." Or, "Who cares?"

Visions can exist at a departmental level as well, bridging individual and organizational visions. A customer service department in a company may choose to pursue a vision of delighted customers. An engineering section may follow a vision of customers well served by great technology.

For leaders, the question is whether the vision is just as attractive as the mission. Is the envisioned result compelling enough to inspire the commitment?

Viktor Frankl once said, "What man actually needs is not a tension-less state but rather the striving and struggling for some goal worthy of him. What he needs is not the discharge of tension at any cost, but the call of a potential meaning waiting to be fulfilled by him."[2]

■ ■ ■ ■ ■ ■   **EXERCISE**
Mission and Vision Statement

Part I. Does your organization have a written mission and vision statement? Do you know it by heart? By its essence?

If there is no written, formal mission and vision statement, what does the work of the organization reveal the operative mission and vision to be? What significant activities reveal the mission and vision?

Part II. What is your gut reaction to the organization's mission and vision statement? What do you feel, at an emotional level, when thinking about the mission and vision? Are they energizing? Motivating? Important to you?

Part III. How do you communicate the mission and vision to others, both inside and outside the organization? What kinds of discussions or stories are conveyed? What is the reaction to these? Is energy created when talking about the mission and vision?

Once one understands the power and relevance of mission and vision for everyone in the workplace—and leaders' roles in articulating, championing, and committing to the mission and vision—it is natural to ask, "Where do mission and vision come from?" In answering, we turn our attention to values.

Values

Underlying the pursuit and connection of mission and vision are values. The word *value* is often misunderstood. It comes from the Latin *valor,* which means "strength." You are strong when you operate out of your own values. Actions corresponding to your values will usually strengthen and reinforce you, wheras actions inconsistent with your values will usually cause confusion and dissipate your energy.

It is crucial for the people in an organization to have a sense of shared values. While it is not possible for any group of people to agree on all values, it is vital that the organization have a critical base of shared, collective values that guide its thinking, actions, decisions, and overall functioning.

Organizations must communicate their values in a genuine way that reflects reality. Employees sometimes express skepticism around their organization's values statements when they sense the organization is talking one thing and doing another—the statements are rightly perceived as hypocritical.

For example, if the official version of an organization's values statement is that customers come first, and the organization routinely shortchanges, misleads, or otherwise neglects customers, cynicism will arise among employees. On the other hand, if the organization makes tough decisions and real sacrifices to take care of customers—

even when it hurts financially—employees will come to understand the very real power of the value placed on putting customers first.

■ ■ ■ ■ ■ ■ **PRINCIPLE**

Organizational values express what is most important along the way to accomplishing the mission.

As a leader, it is important to ensure you are aligned with your organization's values if you want to ensure a commitment on your part. If you disagree with the values, disconnects materialize and will ultimately be obvious to those around you. Lacking the commitment to the organization's values, your leadership will be limited.

■ ■ ■ ■ ■ ■ **PRINCIPLE**

You must genuinely believe in the mission, vision, and values of the organization and find alignment between those and your personal mission, vision, and values in order to do your best work as a leader.

A story wraps up our discussion of all these elements. One participant in a management development program, Jack, once walked into a session and shared what he had seen that morning. Jack, who worked in a workplace safety enforcement role, had driven by a worksite where an employee was not wearing regulation breathing material. Jack was unable to stop and had no actual badge authority on the site anyway, working instead as a manager in his own office in headquarters.

However, Jack related that as he saw this employee breathing dangerous substances, he remembered all the people who were wearing the safety equipment that day as a result of his work in headquarters. He said, "It made me proud that some people are going to live to see their grandchildren because I do what I do each day. Sometimes I forget. But it makes me proud to know I'll make a difference for those people."

Here, Jack talked about a mission (his agency exists to protect workers), vision (healthy workers without a shortened lifespan), and values (caring about workers and their safety).

This story should convey the power this holds. There is no doubt in my mind that Jack is committed to his organization, and I hope he tells that story often to others.

■ ■ ■ ■ ■ **EXERCISE**
Organizational Values

Part I. What are your organization's stated values? How faithfully do the stated values reflect actions and decisions day-to-day in the organization? Is there a tight connection, or are the stated values perceived as "words on paper"?

Part II. Thinking about controversial, difficult, stressful, or painful moments in the organization, did it live its stated values? What can you deduce by objectively observing what happened and then identifying what values were in operation at the time?

■ ■ ■ ■ ■ ■ **PRINCIPLE**

Giving voice to the organization's mission, vision, values, and performance keeps others engaged.

■ ■ **Performance**

Once the organization has a clear sense of mission, vision, and values, it is ready to engage in the next, deeper level of inquiry. It is only after this foundational work is complete that the organization is prepared to assess how it is making good on the promises implied by mission, vision, and values. Being committed to the organization provides the fuel for engaging in this sometimes challenging work.

The fact is, the best of intentions are no guarantee the organization will perform effectively in executing what it wants to get done. You can think of mission, vision, and values as the extremely important prelude to performance. They set the stage. The question is how well the organization then performs.

■ ■ ■ ■ ■   A LEADER'S COMMITMENTS

Joe is sitting tight amid a large-scale reorganization and product-line reconfiguration. Few people seem to know what's coming, and therefore what to do. Keeping the head down seems to be the most common strategy. As a result, Joe sees potentially important information not being exchanged, and ideas that could help in a change effort not getting discussed. For example, clued-in customers seem to be moving away as they sense new risks in doing business with the organization.

Joe's leadership move is to approach his manager, ask what can be shared about direction, and offer the insights. Joe may learn some limited information that helps to engage what is coming. He can also offer to help craft messages that will reassure customers, and facilitate discussions with others at work about how to cope with uncertainty until more can be shared. By disclosing his own feelings of uncertainty to colleagues, coupled with a determination to see the change through, Joe makes it easier for others to talk about their feelings, understand their legitimacy, and find some measure of resolve in navigating the situation.

In doing so, Joe demonstrates leadership commitment to the organization and to people.

A commitment to the organization embraces the work of making a truth-anchored, clear-eyed assessment of how things are going. Leaders champion this work, rather than avoiding it. Lest this sound obvious, recall the fact that a metaphor has arisen for how people avoid the subject. It is called "ignoring the 10,000-pound elephant in the middle of the room."

We offer some specific techniques for engaging these topics, along with how to make good on the commitments.

Making the Commitment to the Organization

So how does a leader demonstrate commitment to the organization?

Mission and vision

Some possibilities for demonstrating commitment to mission and vision include the following:

- Tell stories about times when the mission and vision were evident in action.
- Ask where others see the mission and vision in action.
- Clearly link your and others' work to the mission and vision.
- Talk about how the mission and vision energize you.

Story-telling is an emerging leadership approach. The ability to engage others in a real story with significance and meaning is powerful. People process data and facts, but they *listen* to stories, particularly ones they see you telling with some conviction, emotion, or passion. Not surprisingly, mission, vision, and values fulfillment often are found in stories that motivate and energize others.

But it doesn't have to be just one-way. Talk to others about where and how they see these factors in action, in real work, and be sure the connection between day-to-day work and mission and vision is kept clear. That link provides meaning and significance.

Sometimes I will have a conversation with a client who has been through leadership development work, perhaps a 360 assessment or an interpersonal skills workshop. In talking with him or her months later and hearing stories about transformed relationships, conflict turned into cooperation, or problems solved, it always makes for a great day. Sharing that with others reminds them that they, too, are engaged in that pursuit, and it renews their commitment.

Values

Possibilities for demonstrating commitment to values include:

- Talk with others about times when the organization lived its values through action.
- Talk openly about times when actions did not embody espoused values.
- Share values with customers, suppliers, and partners. Ask what they think, and what their organizations' values are.

Communicating about values can be difficult. Think of values as the part of the iceberg beneath the water-line. Values often are invisible, or unconscious—and that is precisely why talking about them helps reinforce the commitment to them. By surfacing what the organization really cares about, values become more real and can serve as a guide to effective action.

■ ■ ■ ■ ■ A LEADER'S COMMITMENTS

Steven is working 70-hour weeks and has been for months. One project after another seems to stack up right on the heels of one just completed. In his own situation, Steven notices flagging energy, motivation, and quality. As he looks around at his colleagues, he sees much of the same thing.

The group he works with is mainly complaining and engaging in dark humor to cope with the load. More people are getting sick, more often, and as Steven looks out, he detects no let-up in sight. He has heard that one colleague broached the issue with a manager, only to hear, "You've gotta do what you've gotta do."

Steven's leadership move is to approach the manager and ask about his or her read on the group, production rates, and the future. After listening carefully and acknowledging the pressures on that manager, Steven says outright, "I think we're headed for trouble—in terms of quality, turnover, and sustainability. I've seen it happen before in these kinds of situations and I have an idea what we could do. Would you like to hear it?" Steven then pitches a reorganization of the work that will better capitalize on strengths where people work very quickly and effectively, while stating that this cannot be an invitation to load up even more on peoples' plates.

In doing so, he demonstrates a leadership commitment to the self, people, and the organization.

Committed leaders continuously observe values in action vis-à-vis espoused values, and are quick to call out discrepancies. This form of truth-telling keeps the organization faithful to its values.

Knowing the purpose, intended outcomes, and values of the organization, and fully committing to those is an important set of steps. The next step in making a commitment to the organization is conducting an assessment of how well the organization is performing.

Performance

An organization can be assessed through many lenses in its quest to perform. The following are some basic tools.

What is working well

- Engage the organization in appreciative inquiry. http://appreciativeinquiry.case.edu/intro/whatisai.cfm
- Call out examples of the organization operating effectively and powerfully.
- Pay attention to and highlight others' emerging strengths— where work has revealed new areas of competence and effectiveness.
- Decode what is happening in great performance so others understand what the contributing elements are. See if those elements can be reconfigured to create new capabilities.
- Resolve to stay focused on operating from a base of what is successful, using this information to forward the organization's efforts and goals.

These approaches help solidify and preserve success. Many organizations rush past acknowledgment of success because there is usually no shortage of areas needing "fixing." This is a mistake, unless the trouble spots are potentially fatal.

■ ■ ■ ■ ■ ■ **PRINCIPLE**

Commitment to the organization means assessing performance and understanding what is and isn't working well.

The practice of appreciative inquiry provides a structure whereby organizations can decode the elements of success, and thereby expand or extend them. It is a success-based methodology, yet our culture often focuses on gap analysis.

What is true for the organization is also true for individuals. Helping others to see what they do well emboldens and motivates them. We all know the price paid when the only feedback a person receives is in response to problems.

■ ■ **What is not working well**
- ■ Openly acknowledge what is not working well in a constructive, non-judgmental way.
- ■ Probe to understand why these areas exist.
- ■ Understand any patterns that may be revealed by these issues.
- ■ Resolve to at least mitigate problem areas, understanding they may not become sources of strength, but can at least be reduced.

This area is more difficult to broach, but critical as part of a commitment. The keys are self-management, honesty, openness, and a constructive intent as you engage problems and setbacks. Determining the root causes of issues can be a tense, even political, exercise in which defensiveness can emerge. One effective way of dealing with this is to show that you can handle admitting mistakes and failures. This approach makes it safer for others to do the same. Involving others in problem-solving increases their commitment more than simply telling them what to do.

■ ■ ■ ■ ■ **PRACTICE TOOL**
Organizational Assessment

Convene a meeting among those who you believe would be willing to make honest, open contributions to the following discussion, in the form of these questions:

1. As an organization, what are we doing very well? How is this a source of strength for us? What enables this performance? How do we sustain that?

2. As an organization, what are we not doing very well? What are the causes of this, and what can we do to mitigate that?

3. What openings, or possibilities, do we see on the horizon? What changes are coming that the organization can adapt to, and optimize through increased performance?

4. What potential issues do we face? What is on the horizon that might be a concern for the organization?

Openings

- Push for the organization to seize upon openings and opportunities. Highlight the potential.

- Ask others to take part in scanning the environment for openings, and recognize their efforts when they contribute.

- Make scanning for these openings a regular part of meetings at some interval, perhaps monthly or quarterly.

This is inherently a future-facing activity, which can push people out of comfort zones of the known and familiar. It calls for imagining what could be, understanding trends and patterns, and moving to action. It is about creating change.

Potential issues

- Brainstorm with others regarding how to counteract potential issues.
- Develop contingency plans.
- Surface quickly with others any emerging issues and discuss how to respond.

This is a defensive approach, but necessary. Problems and challenges are inevitable, and organizations that can organize around these fastest have an advantage. You can play a role in showing a commitment to the organization in fostering these discussions. Don't be surprised when others see the issues differently. Part of the leadership work is to bring these different voices together in addressing challenges.

Essentially, we have explored the foundations and operation of the organization, and how leaders need to commit to these processes and ways of thinking. It is natural to explore next what can derail any of these commitments.

What Gets in the Way?

There is no shortage of potential detractors to the commitment to the organization. Below, we explore some of the most common.

- Not really believing in the organization or caring how it performs
- Not communicating the mission and other elements

■ Giving the commitment lip service

■ Confusing compliance and commitment

■ Allowing self-interest to trump organizational interest.

Not really believing in the organization or caring how it performs

When we understand all the above, it may seem a bit surprising that a leader might not actually believe in the organization or how it is performing—but think about it: How many times do you see active displays of the commitment? The reality is many leaders have lukewarm to neutral feelings about their organizations, which they see as providing a paycheck.

Unfortunately, the larger the organization, the greater the potential for this. Lost in the feeling of abstraction that huge processes can sometimes engender, a leader may mentally check out and become indifferent to the ultimate aims and performance of the organization.

It is important for leaders to remind themselves regularly what they are contributing to, how that matters for others, and why it's worth it. If they don't think it is, they may feel more fulfilled elsewhere.

Not communicating the mission and other elements

If the commitment is genuinely there, there may be another problem: It just doesn't get discussed much. A leader may have a clear internal sense of it, but doesn't convey it to others. As discussed, it is important for leaders to regularly take opportunities to ensure that others truly understand the intents and purposes of the organization, thereby fostering their own commitment.

Giving the commitment lip service

This may be the most damaging: It is not actually believing in or being committed to the organization, but acting as if you are. This, of course, is the fodder for dark humor aimed at organizational dysfunction, often found in television shows such as "The Office," or the "Dilbert" comic strip. It quickly comes across as duplicitous and flat. It probably reduces whatever motivation may have already been there in others. As expressed above, if you don't actually believe in the organization, you may be more fulfilled elsewhere.

Confusing compliance and commitment

There is a world of difference between compliance and commitment. Compliance usually means going along with the minimum required to get by, whereas commitment represents a genuine interest and energy. Compliance creates token efforts, whereas commitment means people will often go beyond what is expected and find inventive ways to solve problems. The litmus test for a leader is whether he or she is operating out of compliance or commitment. It is difficult to impossible to truly lead others when operating out of a sense of compliance. Others sense it quickly and wonder why *they* should fully commit when a leader hasn't.

Allowing self-interest to trump organizational interest

Self-interest is the engine of capitalism and, in Adam Smith's famous invisible hand metaphor, the mechanism by which everyone supposedly benefits. It is not difficult today to see the limitations of this model generally (sustainability, environmental damage, and corruption), but the engine of self-interest comes to a grinding halt in the realm of leadership.

Leaders simply must elevate organizational interest over their own personal interests if they want the organization to be truly successful. Furthermore, there is no one who waves a magic wand over the heads of leaders and gets them to adopt this new consciousness. Instead, it is a journey that each leader navigates uniquely. The best leaders come to a clear understanding of this very high price.

■ ■ ■ ■ ■ ■ PRINCIPLE

Elevate organizational interest above self-interest.

When a leader's behavior subverts the relationship between organizational interest and self-interest, the rest of the organization detects it almost immediately. The message is broadcast to everyone that "We're all on our own and you had better take care of yourself." While this sounds harsh, it is the felt reality in many organizations.

When the perception is "He's looking out for number one," or "She's taking care of herself," individuals and departments begin to scramble, competing for resources and power.

■ ■ ■ ■ ■ EXERCISE
Self-Interest versus Organizational Interest

Part I. As a leader, in what ways have you subordinated self-interest to serve larger organizational interests? Have you at times allowed your own private interests to get in the way of doing the right thing for the organization?

Part II. Is the culture of your organization one largely of self-interest or organizational interest? In either case, what is the impact?

Some leaders of functional areas or departments do this. These leaders have effectively broken ranks with the whole organization and are simply looking to benefit themselves through the survival and success of their own business function. They have abandoned their commitment to the organization as a whole. When this happens, it becomes difficult to understand an organization in its entirety; in reality, it has become a fragmented set of different business functions.

The written program for a group of children being inducted into the National Junior Honor Society at a middle school in Arlington, Virginia, noted, "The price of leadership is sacrifice—the willingness to yield one's personal interests for the interest of others."

Jim Collins, in his book *Good to Great*, notes that "Level 5 [the most effective] leaders channel their ego needs away from themselves and into the larger goal of building a great company. It's not that Level 5 leaders have no ego or self-interest. Indeed, they are incredibly ambitious but their ambition is first and foremost for the institution, not themselves."[3]

Collins goes on to state: "The great irony is that the animus and personal ambition that often drive people to positions of power stand at odds with the humility required for Level 5 leadership."[4]

No one can subordinate self-interest arbitrarily, or simply on demand. Moreover, there is no mystical process that changes a person's basic motivations when he or she takes a leadership position. Instead, this subordination of self-interest and the consequent commitment to the organization have to make sense in some way.

Perhaps the only real reason for someone to turn away from sole self-interest is that he or she believes that what the organization is accomplishing is worth it. That is, the result of the organization's work is so compelling that the leader is willing to let go of at least some of that pure self-interest and make a true commitment to the organization.

There is also a risk in the other direction. Some leaders so completely identify with their work that they overdo it. This is the path to burnout and exhaustion. Not surprisingly, it is often found in the helping professions. Effective leaders commit to the long haul, not burning out in the process, though the temptations to work harder and longer are many.

Leaders must be committed to their organizations in order to fully align with them and to bring all their mental and emotional resources to the work. The key is the connection between the individual quest for meaning in the form of mission and vision fulfillment, and what the organization is accomplishing.

Leaders who find or create this connection, demonstrate this commitment, and engage others in conversations about the importance of the organization's work help others see the meaning and significance of their efforts. Doing so answers a critical life question practically everyone asks at one time or another: "Why am I here?"

Part of making the commitment—and of making good on it—is the sometimes hard work of honestly assessing how the organization is doing. Truly believing in the organization's work carries the price of reality-checking performance.

Are you committed to your organization?

ENDNOTES

1. Henry Mintzberg, "Enough Leadership," *The Harvard Business Review,* November 2004, 22.
2. Viktor Frankl, *Man's Search for Meaning* (New York: Washington Square Press, Simon and Schuster, 1963), 166.
3. Jim Collins, *Good to Great: Why Some Companies Make the Leap . . . and Others Don't* (New York: HarperBusiness, 2001), 21.
4. Ibid., 36.

RECOMMENDED READING

Senge, Peter. *The Fifth Discipline.* New York: Doubleday, 1990.

Wheatley, Margaret. *Leadership and the New Science.* New York: Berrett Koehler, 1992.

Zander, Benjamin, and Rosamund Zander. *The Art of Possibility.* Boston: Harvard Business School Press, 2000.

4 A Commitment to the Truth

"I never did give them hell. I just told the truth, and they thought it was hell."

—HARRY TRUMAN

Approaching the subject of truth-telling in organizations today can be unsettling or uncomfortable. The phrase itself may sound a little high-minded, or perhaps quaint.

Some leaders may think it would be nice in a perfect world, and then remind us of pressing realities: competitive pressures, colliding objectives, and relentless demands to just get things done. Speaking the truth can threaten those objectives. As a result, some people consider the phrase "truth-telling in organizations" to be an oxymoron because they feel that their organizations have made it profoundly threatening to tell the truth.

However, leaders must give voice to the truth. They must be committed to the truth in order for the organization to do its best work. This means understanding the truth, surfacing the truth, and sharing the truth with others. Working from false assumptions, misinformation, or denial is a recipe for misalignment and incoherence in work. Accountability and commitment to the truth are fundamental, sometimes painful, and always inescapable.

The promise is that truth-telling helps the organization to detect, learn, respond well to a variety of events, communicate effectively, and align itself with customers' real needs. It helps leaders at all levels to be a critical part of that.

▪ ▪ ▪ ▪ ▪ ▪ PRINCIPLE

As a leader, you must be a truth-teller—a model. You cannot lead people if you do not tell them the truth.

▪ ▪ ▪ What Is a Commitment to the Truth?

Being committed to the truth as a leader means engaging on three crucial levels: with yourself, with others, and with the organization at large.

The pursuit of the truth about yourself—self-awareness, in particular—is the essence of being committed to yourself as a leader. It is an internal truth that results from a kind of internal communication.

Realizing you may have consciously or unconsciously deluded yourself on an issue that you had a strong interest in is an example of this.
In such a case you may have learned something about yourself that
resulted from telling yourself the truth: that you did not pay much attention to information that was contrary to how you were seeing the
situation. The learning that results from this internal truth-telling
is to be sure to check next time you feel very strongly invested in a
particular outcome.

■ ■ ■ ■ ■ ■ **PRINCIPLE**

Truth-telling occurs on the level of the self, with others, and
within the organization.

Truth-telling with others takes the shape of honest external communication. This keeps the air clear, keeps everyone in the loop, reduces
misinformation, and minimizes perception errors. An example of
truth-telling is when you admit a mistake, particularly one that affected someone else negatively. The mistake could take the form of
having overlooked another's interests in a situation, or not having
taken into account another's goals in making a decision. We all make
lapses like these. Truth-telling with another improves the relationship and environment. It need not be anchored in the self; it may simply be sharing information about external conditions—what's going
well, and what isn't, for example.

Truth-telling in the organization at large means surfacing what needs
to be communicated across groups of people—in teams, workgroups,
or operating units, for example. This is a pivotal point at which leaders emerge—by saying what needs to be said for the good of the organization (reflecting a commitment to the organization). A person
who does not rise to meet the challenge of leadership "goes to ground"

by playing safe and withholding the potentially controversial ideas that could move the organization closer to the truth about what it should be doing. An example of true leadership is stepping up when you think the organization is headed down the wrong path, saying the truth as you see it. Perhaps a marketing strategy is not unfolding as was planned, but others are reluctant to speak up about it. It could be an IT group in conflict with the customer service function. Sometimes the truth-telling may be conveying to each group what it needs to hear and understand about the other group's perceptions.

■ ■ ■ ■ ■ **EXERCISE**
Hard Truths About the Self, Others, and the Organization

Part I. What hard truths have you told yourself about you? When was the last time you did so? Have you avoided admitting the truth to yourself? What have you learned through truth-telling about yourself? Have others given you difficult feedback you did not accept?

Part II. What hard truths have you told others? When was the last time you did so? Have you avoided truth-telling to others? What have you successfully helped others learn about themselves through such truth-telling?

Part III. What hard truths have you told throughout the organization, or at least your particular part of the organization? When was the last time you did so? Have you avoided organizational truth-telling? What have you successfully helped the organization learn through such truth-telling?

■ ■ ■ Types of Truth

It is important to distinguish among three basic types of truth: preferences, facts, and conclusions.

Preferences exist independently of the truth. It's a fact (and true) that you like some things and dislike others. For example, you like some aspects of your job more than others. It's not right or wrong. It just is.

Facts can be verified or disproved. They are the easiest type of truth to ascertain and come to agreement on. The facts are indispensable in discerning the truth about decisions and choices. Sometimes people will say things like, "It's a fact that we should do this," but this confuses fact with the next category—conclusions.

Conclusions are the same as opinions or inferences, and this is where most of the conversation occurs in organizations. Conclusions come from answering questions such as "What is the best thing to do?" or "How should we move ahead?" With this kind of information, the truth will be knowable to different degrees—it may be easily validated and clear to see, or it might be much more controversial and unclear. Different individuals will feel different individual truths, based on their perceptions, experiences, and frames of reference. While it is a fact that you may feel a particular way, it doesn't mean you're necessarily right. Your felt truth may be off target. There may be facts you don't have. However, openly and constructively sharing those individual, and sometimes competing, truths can have powerful results as the collective information becomes richer, more multifaceted and wide-ranging.

Understanding these distinctions, let's look at the state of truth-telling in organizations today.

Truth-telling Today

The reason the topic of truth in organizations has an "edge" to it for many people is that they think it's getting short-shrift.

Data from the Office of Personnel Management in the federal government indicate that fewer than half of employees feel their organizations' leaders maintain high standards of honesty and integrity.

What's more, this perception has been consistent over several years—it is not a statistical departure from norm.[1]

It goes to the highest levels. A Gallup poll in 2007 found that the most important quality voters are seeking in the next U.S. president is honesty. In fact, about twice as many respondents identified honesty to be the most important quality as those who placed leadership itself at the top.[2]

In their book *The Leadership Challenge,* Kouzes and Posner write: "In every survey we conducted, honesty was selected more often than any other leadership characteristic; it consistently emerged as the single most important ingredient in the leader-constituent relationship."[3]

If you have been in an organization where the truth was compromised, then you already know the results when the workforce learns what has happened. It is demotivating and demoralizing to most people.

One leader related a story to me of his first job out of college with a real-estate company. He was excited and motivated. One day he was instructed to put up in a subdivision a large sign that proclaimed, "Only a few homes left!" He knew not one had been sold. He never felt the same about the company, and he ultimately quit. When the truth gets sacrificed, so do the quality and durability of leaders' relationships with others, putting everything else in work at risk.

For leaders, the stakes are high. Perceptions of withholding, fudging, or avoiding the truth are quick to form—and then difficult to shift. They erode credibility and confidence, and they tend to set into motion self-protecting, dysfunctional behavior. Communication is damaged, trust declines, and disclosure becomes dangerous. Who wants to tell the truth when that is not valued in an organization?

In addition, there are repercussions for the business. James G. Clawson, in his book *Level 3 Leadership,* writes: " ... if potential leaders cannot create an atmosphere around them in which others are encouraged to tell the truth and find it safe to do so, the business will be making decisions based on late or faulty or incomplete information far too often."[4]

■ ■ ■ ■ ■ ■ **PRINCIPLE**

Truth-telling creates a "true north" that is critical for organizational performance.

When people lack a clear and accurate context in which to act appropriately, they have limited ideas about—and a fragmented understanding of—what is happening. This means their understanding is flawed, and the quality of their decisions is consequently poor.

But there is a much more positive alternative, and it is the outcome of a commitment to the truth.

Trust, candor, effective problem-solving, and collaboration result from truth-telling and truth-sharing. You have no doubt dealt with people who told it straight—gave you the pluses and minuses, so that you could make a good decision. In all probability, you considered these people true partners and were more willing to entrust them with an influence in big decisions.

Apart from any ethical, social, or moral considerations, the business case matters. In a knowledge or idea economy, the creation of maximum value hinges on empowerment through accurate information. People *need* the truth to ensure their work is aimed in the right direction. For example, disclosing difficult problems the organization is facing will generally get people thinking about how to solve them.

■ ■ ■ ■ ■ **PRACTICE TOOL**
Discerning the Truth Amid Opinions

In the next conflict or difference of opinion you encounter, practice the following technique to help discern the basis for different views:

Part I. What do we each know? What is provable?

Part II. How do our facts differ? How does that potentially explain the difference in conclusions reached?

Part III. What reasoning process did we each use to come to our conclusions? How did we move from facts to conclusions? What was solid or weak in our respective reasoning processes? Where did we each make assumptions or make large inductive leaps?

Part IV. Based on this analysis, which perspective is probably closer to the truth, inasmuch as we can now see that? If we can't, what additional information do we now need?

The truth serves as a kind of "true north" against which experience, problems, interactions, and indeed all activities can be understood. It is the plumb line indicating what is real.

In contrast to the negative feeling created when the truth is compromised, there is an exciting sense that new ground is broken when the truth is spoken. There's a feeling of moving forward in a positive direction. Consistent, clear truth-telling frees up enormous energy in an organization.

■ ■ ■ ■ ■ ■ **PRINCIPLE**

Consistent, clear truth-telling frees up enormous energy in an organization.

Clawson writes, "Although it may seem trite to say that truth telling is a moral foundation for effective leadership, I find that not all managers or would-be leaders believe in truth telling. . . . The truth, as you see it and communicate it to others, is a great crucible that burns out would-be leaders and hardens effective and true leaders. . . . If you are unwilling to tell people the truth, you will not be able to lead them. . . . It refines relationships by cleaning out hidden goals, ulterior motives, suppressed resentments, manufactured conclusions, and uncertainties about the values of the other person."[5]

Stated simply, a commitment to the truth raises the game. It makes work *better.*

Making the Commitment to the Truth

If we accept the hard premise that telling the truth is actually worth it, the question then becomes: What can you as a leader do to promote truth-telling among others and throughout the organization?

Model the behavior

The most important action is to model the behavior. Like so many other things, that's easier said than done, particularly when performance isn't happening, a much-anticipated initiative is faltering, or something you actively supported turns out to be a bad idea. But it's worth it.

As Dotlich and Cairo state in their book, *Why CEOs Fail*, "... if top people are open and honest about their flaws, they will help create a culture of openness and honesty."[6]

I remember becoming angry with a colleague over a decision once, and my boss finding out about it. He asked me, very calmly and openly, what had happened, and I'm sure I replied in a rationalizing, self-justifying and defensive way, keeping the focus on the bad decision my counterpart had made. He quietly said, "One thing I've realized too many times is that every time I speak to someone out of anger I regret it later."

My manager disclosing his own mistakes in this area made it easier for me to admit the truth: I had lost my temper.

"Humility leads to strength and not to weakness. It is the highest form of self-respect to admit mistakes and to make amends for them."

—John J. McCloy

This manager also embodied another aspect of modeling the behavior. He delivered the information in a way that recognized my feelings. That was actually the key to the effectiveness of it. Truth-telling without considering how it will be heard or felt can be brutal, and counterproductive. This relates to being committed to people.

At the Shambhala Institute, where an annual conference attracts the leading thinkers in leadership development, such as Peter Senge, Margaret Wheatley, and Julio Olalla, great emphasis is put on leader humanness and even vulnerability. In the Shambhala tradition, a leader's demonstration of vulnerability, perhaps through admitting a mistake or weakness, invites others into the creation of a new, resonant, and authentic field. In this field, it is considered wise and responsible to talk about what is not going well.

This leads us to the next practice.

Make it safe to tell the truth

Making it safe to tell the truth means not shooting down anyone bearing unwelcome news or unpopular perspectives. Even if you disagree with the information, make it a point to listen and understand first. Telling one's truth and listening to another's truth does not mean that everyone will always agree, but it does mean that everyone's best contributions will make it into the discussion. Simple phrases like, "We may not all agree on everything said, but it needs to be said and understood if we are to do our best work," will convey volumes about your intent.

Again, from a business-case perspective, note that significant change can only come out of divergent ideas. Making truth-telling dangerous can reinforce the status quo just when change may be needed.

At the level of the self, realize some of the truth-telling may be about you. Particularly when you have done something and were not aware of the negative impact, it can be hard to hear the truth. This is a classic conflict scenario. James Clawson writes in *Level 3 Leadership*: "The challenge for the person listening to another's truth-telling is to remain non-defensive with ears and heart open, listening carefully to what is being communicated. Too often, people begin to get defensive immediately and miss the main message or its meaning."[7]

Making it safe for others to tell the truth is a big step, and you can go even further by intentionally inviting them to step into that space.

Invite and ask others for their truths

Another way to promote truth-telling is to intentionally ask people about the lessons they learned after any significant experience. Give them time to prepare their views in advance so they can think through carefully how they really think and feel. As they hear different takes on what mattered and what happened, they will increase their appreciation of the diversity of views. Again, individuals' felt truths may vary, and the idea is that by sharing those different perspectives a powerful shared understanding can be built.

▪ ▪ ▪ ▪ ▪ ▪ PRINCIPLE

You must make it safe for, and invite, others to tell the truth.

Again, this is not code for accepting all conclusions, regardless of merit. In fact, part of the practice should include critical thinking skills that allow the group to get to the bottom of issues and ideas, sifting fact from opinion, grounded conclusions from more spurious ones. This should be done in a constructive way that helps everyone sharpen and refine their thinking for the next time.

The analysis tools presented in this chapter of commitment to the organization are also an opportunity to surface truth-telling. The real test comes in describing areas where performance is poor, or emerging challenges. You will find that when you talk frankly and constructively about problems in the organization, it will invite others to do so, too.

> #### ■ ■ ■ ■   A LEADER'S COMMITMENTS
>
> A competitor has launched an impressive new product. As a member of the product development team, Michael has seen the positive reception given to the competitor's product in the press and among customers. He is also aware of the internal team conditions within his organization that seemed to slow down progress and stall an earlier release that could have competed with the product the competitor just launched.
>
> As the team discusses the new product, Michael notices that a few very vocal members trash it. They point to what seem to Michael to be very minor points in functionality that he does not believe are significant to customers. Others are much quieter amid the discussion.
>
> Michael's leadership move is to say, "I realize this may be difficult, but my own perception is that this product is doing well. I believe the key features being used the most by customers are what's important. But whatever the competition has done, I think the bigger issue for us now is what we are going to do. My sense is that we need to understand how we lost time, and ultimately, what our next move is with our own product. That is one opinion on this, and I'd like to hear what others think, particularly if that has not already been expressed."
>
> In doing this, Michael demonstrates a leadership commitment to people, the organization, and the truth.

Good, open-ended questions tend to promote truth-telling more than pronouncements or judgments. Questions you can ask to promote truth-telling include:

- ■ What are we seeing and what might we be missing?
- ■ Where have we gotten it right and wrong?
- ■ Is there anything we are doing that makes telling the truth hard? Is there anything I am doing?

The answers should be discussed in a way that looks like a conversation rather than competing monologues, rigidly fixed positions, or ideologies.

Confront reality

Both Jim Collins, in his book, *Good to Great,* and Sidney Finkelstein, in his book, *Why Smart Executives Fail,* stress the importance of paying attention to surprises and negative information, communicating openly about them, and then acting wisely. In contrast to the humorous bumper sticker, denial is not an option.

Collins writes: "All good to great companies began the process of finding a path to greatness by confronting the brutal facts of their current reality. When you start with an honest and diligent effort to determine the truth of your situation, the right decisions often become self-evident. It is impossible to make good decisions without infusing the entire process with an honest confrontation of the brutal facts. A primary task in taking a company from good to great is to create a culture wherein people have a tremendous opportunity to be heard and, ultimately, for the truth to be heard. One of the primary ways to demotivate people is to ignore the brutal facts of reality."[8]

■ ■ ■ ■ ■ EXERCISE
Truth-Telling in the Organizational Culture

On a scale of 1–10, with 10 being a completely honest or truthful culture, how would you characterize your organization? What are the implications for high levels of truth-telling or truth-withholding? Have you seen people punished for telling the truth? What was the impact on the culture?

This stepping up to, and into, problems is a strong demonstration of a commitment to the truth.

▦ ▦ Access intuition and emotion

Even in our hyper-rational world, leaders need to remain in touch with their intuition and emotions—those sometimes subtle guides to unconscious signals that something needs to be said—and to encourage others to do the same. One way to do this is to ask members in a meeting what their gut is telling them, particularly about important decisions. Leadership coaches sometimes ask clients what they are feeling at that exact moment. The truth that emerges from such questions tends to help create clarity.

■ ■ ■ ■ ■   A LEADER'S COMMITMENTS

Sally is in a meeting where another department conducts an elaborate presentation on a new internal process for managing cost. The software to be used is very expensive, ironically, and Sally saw it fail spectacularly in a previous organization where she worked.

Sally notices that any questions about the efficacy of the software are met with thinly disguised defensiveness and hostility by the project champions.

Sally's leadership move is to choose to not engage the subject at that time, when emotions are already on edge. Instead, she sits down with the project lead over coffee and offers to share what she learned using the software previously. She is careful to not outright attack the project, but to acknowledge what seem to be good points along with the reality of what she experienced. Sally also remains open to the possibility that her perceptions may now be outdated—bug fixes and newer versions may have ironed out the problems. Until that is determined, Sally offers to help the project lead look carefully at the areas of concern, maintaining a non-confrontational and supportive attitude throughout. Further, by empathizing with the concerns and fears the project lead may now be feeling, she makes it easier for that lead to talk openly about anything that may be awry.

In doing so, Sally has demonstrated a leadership commitment to people, the organization, and the truth.

You have probably had the experience of sitting in a meeting where things were headed in a direction you didn't feel was right. Perhaps you sat quietly, running a calculation on the risks and rewards of speaking up. In that same meeting, you may have heard someone else finally broach what you felt needed to be said.

Two things can happen in such cases: Either everyone goes to ground waiting for the adverse reaction from whoever is in power in the room, or, if the climate is more open, there is a noticeable shift of energy in the room as participants realize the undeniable. You will often see clear nonverbal signals of acceptance of the truth as people vigorously nod their heads, make affirming gestures, or even say "Yes!" as the truth is laid out. This is part of the energy released when the truth shows up. In such a case, the person who spoke up acted like a real leader, demonstrating a commitment to the truth.

It should be clear that voicing the truth is important, but isn't always demonstrated. This takes us to the subject of what gets in the way.

■ ■ ■ ■ ■   **PRACTICE TOOL**
Surfacing Others' Truths

Part I. While discussing any issue, if you feel others might be holding back their own felt truths, whether out of fear, anxiety, or any other factor, ask the group, "Are there any other perspectives we should consider?" This is neutral language that invites other ideas.

Part II. Particularly if the room goes quiet, surface explicitly the point of view you suspect may be held, but which has not yet been surfaced. Check with others to see if any feel this way. It may be just what is needed to open up a new perspective.

What Gets in the Way?

While there is basically one way to tell the truth (perhaps with some variations around degrees of diplomacy, tact, and sensitivity), there are myriad creative ways to not tell it.

Manipulating information

Often, the truth gets lost or muddied as a result of an extensive and clever process of massage and manipulation, with selected, hand-picked facts arranged just so. We hear of the need to "frame the message" and "stay on message." While there is nothing wrong with clearly organizing and presenting information, it can be a cover for manipulating the information. We also hear about "bending" the truth, "massaging" the numbers, telling a "white lie," or "being a little creative" with the figures. An entire vocabulary has arisen to mentally and emotionally protect us from the harsh reality that the truth is sometimes on the run.

Statistics are often manipulated to present the desired picture. Whether it is selecting a convenient subset of the data—those that most powerfully support your position—or ignoring contradicting data, there are many ways to step aside from the central, unvarnished truth.

Withholding information

It's usually not about outright lying—much more often, it's about selective withholding of the truth. Individuals and entire departments routinely withhold information from each other so they don't appear wrong or vulnerable.

Many leaders stage-manage presentations to employees to maintain a perception that they are invulnerable and all is well. Of course, the opposite approach is to openly and candidly discuss both what is going well and what is not going well. Where this doesn't happen, it is clear that asking a hard question may result in being branded "not a team player," or a trouble-maker. This is why many employees bring a mentality of "pay no attention to that man behind the curtain" to large corporate events where they are given a sanitized version of reality.

The courtroom charge is to tell the truth, the whole truth, and nothing but the truth. Partial truth doesn't count.

Why the Truth Isn't Told

There are several very powerful motivators for people not giving full expression to the truth.

Belief in needing to do whatever it takes

I'll never forget learning that one small company I worked for had fudged some numbers in order to show the parent company that it had met its revenue goals. The game every month was the same: While we talked endlessly about strategy and marketing plans, all that really mattered was the bottom line. With the temerity of a very young member of the workforce, I told the CEO what I had heard and asked him what had happened. Since the entire executive team knew what had happened, he must have felt it didn't matter if others knew; it was bound to get out. He said, with a straight face (and pride), "What we did took great courage and cunning."

That's one way to look at it: Falsifying information and doing whatever it takes to succeed (at least on paper) takes a kind of courage. The effect, however, was instantly demotivating.

> ■ ■ ■ ■ ■   **PRACTICE TOOL**
> Advocacy and Truth-Telling
>
> The next time you are advocating for a position you strongly believe in—a result you really want—stop and ask yourself before presenting your case:
>
> 1.   Have I included all the relevant information, or just the information that tends to support my position?
>
> 2.   Do I accurately describe competing points of view, or do I minimize or brush them aside?
>
> 3.   Why is it that I want this result so strongly?

Finkelstein also writes, for example, of how the pressure to make earnings targets was so intense at some failed companies that some executives simply provided good quarterly numbers whether they were true or not.

Indeed, the emphasis on "doing whatever it takes" to achieve an objective has become a dominant force in our culture, to the extent that breaches of ethics, the law, or simply the truth are not only widespread, but they are also often acknowledged and uncomfortably filed away as part of the price of doing business. Companies routinely pay "settlements" to federal agencies for breaking the law. They do not have to admit wrongdoing, but pay the settlement so they "can get on with the business of serving customers." This tidy arrangement institutionalizes withholding the truth.

Unless a truth-telling culture is intentionally forged, people have a tendency to package information in a way that makes them look good, and they avoid saying difficult things that will upset others.

Loyalty

We often avoid the truth when our behavior or thinking, if exposed, would be embarrassing or compromising. Sherron Watkins, vice president of corporate development at Enron, sent CEO Kenneth Lay a six-page memo before the company's fall, laying out what she saw and her concerns over what could happen. For her efforts at truth-telling, she was branded a traitor and disloyal to the organization.

Employees often develop a finely tuned sense of what is safe to say based on leaders' reactions to any communication that appears to test the existing order and interests. These reactions are usually not in words; more often they take the form of facial expressions, body language, or eye contact. The message definitely gets delivered. When it is expressed verbally, it may take the form of something like, "I wouldn't say anything about that if I were you."

Many whistleblowers have had their lives turned upside down by telling the truth. Some organizations today value accomplishing something, and making money, over being honest and telling the truth. This is exactly why truth-telling sounds a bit old-fashioned in modern times.

Some leaders continue to operate on the implicit basis that might makes right, and that talking about negative things will only weaken the organization. But employees know that might will never make the truth.

To avoid internal discomfort

One reason for not telling the truth that many people can relate to was memorialized in the famous scene from the movie *A Few Good*

Men, when Jack Nicholson bellowed at Tom Cruise: "You can't handle the truth!"

The discomfort can come from many sources—other individuals, departments, or even customers.

For example, organizations can characterize their customers in a way that makes it easy to keep uncomfortable, critical information at arms' length. When the customer wants something that the organization cannot do, or criticizes some work the organization has done, the response is often to attack the customer for being unreasonable, having artificially high expectations, or operating in bad faith. The severity of the attack usually correlates with the degree of vulnerability the organization feels.

I experienced an example of this a few years ago when a company I was working for rolled out a new software product. We found it hard to learn, use, or even understand. We began to show it to customers, patiently explaining its key features and functionality. Unfortunately, our explanations did not seem to provide what the customers needed to use the software effectively. We also began hearing from our colleagues in the sales department that their prospects were resisting the new product because it was difficult to use.

It came to a head at the U.S. Treasury, when a senior-level executive walked into a meeting and said, "I'll be brief. Your product is hard to use, it takes us too long to find what we need, and it's not intuitive. I'm not the only one who thinks this; it's everyone I've talked to."

We limped out of that meeting after promising more training and went to New York, where the verdict from Wall Street customers was also now coming in. After hearing the caustic comments from razor-sharp bond traders and a Senior Executive Service leader at Treasury, one executive in our company said, "Well, the customers are stupid."

This staggering response kept the truth about the failure to truly understand needs and preferences at bay, shifting the blame to the people paying our salaries.

■ ■ ■ ■ ■   **PRACTICE TOOL**
External Perspectives

Ask your customers, suppliers, partners, and others with insight into your organization and/or its services or products to tell you some truths that they imagine the organization may both want and not want to hear. What convergence is there between your perception of the organization and others' perceptions?

Conflict is a prime example of where discomfort can operate to keep the truth suppressed. In a conflict situation, how open can you remain, for how long, to what the other person is actually saying? How long can you stay open to the possibility that there is some truth in what he or she is saying? Try this on yourself in the next meeting you're in where conflict emerges. Emotions often prompt an immediate shutdown. Instead of trying to discover the truth, countermeasures are unleashed.

Finkelstein writes about fear and concealing the truth: "Do these problems sound exaggerated? Isn't the idea of a company suppressing critical data a little farfetched? We saw it happen in case after case that we studied. At microchip manufacturer Advanced Micro Devices (AMD), for example, employees were so careful to maintain a positive attitude when dealing with CEO Jerry Sanders that he never heard about the serious delays plaguing the manufacture of the company's crucial K5 chip. Even when the problems became increasingly obvious at the lower levels, each level in the management hierarchy struggled to put a positive spin on what it was hearing from below. Eventually, as one former employee said, 'Everyone in the company knew the thing was in bad shape but Jerry,' the CEO."[9]

He states further that "People will avoid mentioning unsettling information or ideas because bringing up such things sounds negative. No one wants to be 'the nitpicker.' There is no reassurance to counter an employee's natural reluctance to be the bearer of bad news. When a company habitually assigns blame for failures, no one is going to speak up when he or she spots a problem."[10]

These examples all point to the need to forge a truth-telling culture, in which mistakes and setbacks can be mined for learning and change.

To avoid demotivating others

Some leaders feel the truth will discourage or demotivate the troops. Almost always, employees ultimately figure out the truth, and by then they have developed a new level of skepticism and distrust in their leaders. Withholding the truth to avoid discouragement is patronizing to adults whose careers and fates hinge on the effectiveness of the organization.

Money

I was at a trade show once when Peter, a colleague, was demonstrating a product to a prospect. The prospect asked a question about the product's capabilities, and Peter answered in a way that seemed general. I knew that the answer to the question was "no," but Peter managed to string together a few sentences that left the opposite impression. The prospect, perhaps sensing the lack of definitiveness in Peter's answer, pressed further, sharpening the question. Peter stayed the course and affirmed that the product would indeed do what the prospect needed. He did this while turning around 180 degrees to face me, and he made his reply with a huge, exaggerated wink.

Of course, all Peter really wanted to do was make the sale. He was aware he was telling a flat-out lie, and apparently he thought his attempt at humor would help him cover his tracks—at least with a colleague.

Generally speaking, as the stakes rise, so do the temptations to withhold or "manage" the truth. Leaders can reflect on whether they outright deceive or more subtly withhold the truth as the financial benefits of doing so rise, and reflect upon the short- and long-run consequences of doing that.

There will never be any shortage of motivations to compromise the truth, but leaders should understand both the negative consequences of doing so, particularly in the long run, and the positive consequences of openly sharing and promoting the truth.

You cannot lead people without telling them the truth, and so a commitment to the truth is essential to lead. Are you committed to the truth?

ENDNOTES

1. The U.S. Office of Personnel Management, http://www.fhcs2006.opm.gov/Reports/ResponseWPCT.asp?AGY=ALL&SECT=4 (accessed April 12, 2008).
2. The Gallup Organization, http://www.gallup.com/poll/27085/Wanted-Next-President-Honesty-Strong-Leadership.aspx (accessed April 12, 2008).
3. James Kouzes and Barry Posner, *The Leadership Challenge* (San Francisco: Jossey-Bass 1995), 22.

4. James Clawson, *Level Three Leadership: Getting Below the Surface* (Upper Saddle River, NJ: Prentice Hall, 1999), 47.

5. Ibid., 46–47.

6. David Dotlich and Peter Cairo, *Why CEOs Fail: The 11 Behaviors That Can Derail Your Climb to the Top and How to Manage Them* (New York: John Wiley & Sons, Inc., 2003), 148.

7. Clawson, 47.

8. Jim Collins, *Good to Great: Why Some Companies Make the Leap.... and Others Don't* (New York: HarperBusiness, 2001), 88–89.

9. Sydney Finkelstein, *Why Smart Executives Fail: And What You Can Learn From Their Mistakes* (New York: Penguin Group, 2003), 177.

10. Ibid., 176.

RECOMMENDED READING

Chaffee, John. *The Thinker's Way.* Boston: Little, Brown and Co., 1998.

Pirsig, Robert. *Zen and the Art of Motorcycle Maintenance.* New York: Morrow Quill, 1974.

The Arbinger Institute. *Leadership and Self-Deception.* San Francisco: Berrett-Koehler, 2002.

5 A Commitment to Leadership

■ ■ ■ ■ ■ ■ ■ ■ ■ ■

"The quality of leadership, more than any other single factor,
determines the success or failure of an organization."

—FRED FIEDLER AND MARTIN CHEMERS

It is only after the individual has made a commitment to the organization, to the people, to the truth, and to the self that he or she is in a position to truly consider what a commitment to leadership means. A person can have the previous four commitments and yet not be committed to leadership. There is one more piece to the puzzle, one more step in the journey.

▪ ▪ ▪ **What Is a Commitment to Leadership?**

The essence of the commitment to leadership is a type of calling. This call may be experienced as a tug of conscience, the insight that a group of people need organizing help to most effectively realize their vision or accomplish their mission. There must be a genuine, felt sense of creating something meaningful through exercising leadership. Only you can determine if leadership is a calling for you. Committing to leadership means committing to this calling.

▪ ▪ ▪ ▪ ▪ ▪ **PRINCIPLE**

Choosing to lead others means answering an internal call to do so.

Not everyone is meant to lead. While it is true that everyone leads in some capacity in his or her own life, at the minimum, only when an individual feels this inner sense of the need to step up should he or she engage in the quest to lead others.

▪ ▪ ▪ ▪ ▪ **EXERCISE**
Answering a Call

Have you felt a "call"—an urge or imperative—to lead others? How did this manifest? How have you acted on or resisted that call?

The importance and strength of this inner voice is revealed in the case of some American Indian tribes, where the call to lead was experienced as an unwelcome, onerous responsibility. In this case, leadership was exercised much more out of a sense of obligation or duty than for any particular individual benefits it created.

■ ■ ■ Making the Commitment to Leadership

With an understanding of the commitments, and now the commitment to leadership, the question becomes: How do you do it? What does it look like? What needs to happen?

Of course, the first step is to choose to make the commitments. Out of this intention the following actions will help you develop your own leadership. Conversely, specific action steps may seem hollow or lackluster without the commitment powering them.

There are two categories of actions to demonstrate and make good on the commitment to leadership. The first is in what you actually do as a leader, and the second is how you get better at that.

■ ■ ■ Exercising Leadership

The following approach to exercising leadership is something of a cycle, and yet leadership could occur at any discrete point in that cycle. Different people could exercise leadership at different points in this cycle. Some points could be omitted, depending on the situation in which the leadership is occurring.

Central to the concept of this cycle is that leadership results in something new—even if that is a validation or confirmation of the status quo. The essence of leadership is that it forwards or advances things in some way. Leadership is often contrasted with management, which administers or preserves what is. Here, leadership as a catalyst is part of creating the future that is perceived as good or better.

■ ■ ■ ■ ■ ■ PRINCIPLE

> Leaders lead by engaging in the system through noticing what is happening and creating change where needed.

There is also an emphasis on leadership actually *doing* something, but this could also be thinking. The action here could be to create new ideas, which might later lead to visible action. People sometimes talk about thought leadership, for example.

Making the commitment to leadership can involve the following:

- Seeing
- Imagining
- Aligning
- Working
- Adapting
- Achieving
- Celebrating
- Seeing anew.

Let's explore each, and see how leadership shows up. Notice how leadership could show up from any source, from any person.

Seeing

Seeing involves observing what is happening now. It means "getting" what is occurring in the organization, others, or the self. It is pure perception, anchored in clear, realistic, and honest insight into conditions. It can take place by witnessing something, having a conversation, or simply noticing. It answers the question: What is happening?

Seeing clearly is a leadership imperative. Not being committed to leadership and not bothering to pay attention to workplace conditions alters the entire trajectory of work. This is the infamous case of repeating chronic problems with no awareness of what they are or why they matter. It could also be not bothering to notice an opportunity. Call it obliviousness. Seeing is part of a commitment to the self, people, the organization, and the truth. Developing your own powers of perception is invaluable.

For example, a leader might fully notice that customers are not often happy with an organization's services, and that there seems to be some strong negative emotion about that within the organization. Rather than deny or overlook that, blame it on the customers, or otherwise sidestep it, a leader would fully recognize and address the situation.

Imagining

Imagining goes beyond a clear recognition of current reality to what could be. Observing what is and then doing nothing is one of the first posts at which leadership can fail. Imagining is visualizing, looking beyond, glimpsing possibility, dreaming, or mentally creating a new situation, structure, or event. It is building in the mind through mental reconfiguration the desired future. It is cognitive and emotional creating. There is a new idea, and positive emotion, motivation behind it.

Imagining is part of the commitment to the self, people, and the organization. That commitment fuels imagining; it provides the energy charge that sparks the thinking, because you care about making things better in the organization.

For example, a leader might wonder about what it would look like to have delighted customers, or perhaps more modestly what a reduction in dissatisfaction might be like. Ideas about both the outcome and how it could be accomplished are firing. This is an inherently creative stage.

Aligning

Aligning means moving from thought to the first stages of action. Here, the leadership move is to communicate with others. There are obviously many ways this could happen, but at the core, a new conversation will be sparked. Something that has not been said will now be introduced. This is to connect with and engage others in the pursuit of something better. You can think of it as enrolling enthusiastic collaborators, motivating and inviting them into something new and exciting.

In a sense, it is "selling" the idea, but it may also be simply getting their perceptions, sharing yours, and forging a shared understanding out of which others will do the imagining. This is letting them take the pride of ownership of the ideas. It doesn't mean you didn't have any, but the move to avoid is showing up with all the answers, trying to organize others around that, and then wondering why they don't seem as motivated as they would be if they had some authorship.

As the shared understanding emerges, plans are made to align around that. The aligning is figuring out who can do what that is different and new in some way, in the pursuit of the better reality. There is often great energy present here, and a leader can help marshal or steward that energy.

Aligning hinges on a commitment to people, truth, and leadership, with people much more likely to respond if the right relationship and conditions have been fostered. It is in the aligning stage that the new forms of leadership really show up. The communication is not command and control, but enroll; it is based not on power or title, but on the engagement around the excitement of creating something new that matters both to the work and to the pride and motivation of the person doing the work.

"Leadership is based on inspiration, not domination; on cooperation, not intimidation."

—William Arthur Wood

For example, a leader may have coffee or a meeting with others to ask how they see things, share what he or she sees, ask what they think would be better, and share his or her own perspective. This is true dialogue, real conversation. This done, the work would turn to making truly collaborative decisions about what can be changed, and how, to secure the desired future: satisfied customers. Perhaps the plan could include helping others learn about empathy, or giving them more autonomy to make customers happy.

Working

Working means the execution. This is the doing, acting, stepping out, and changing what happens. This is where the creative processes become real in work. Roles, tasks, and practices are different now. Something new is happening. It's where rubber meets road. Who does the work can be configured many different ways, but the old leadership view of doing all the thinking and then others all the implementing is not part of the plan. Leaders may work as peers, even subordinates. Whoever is doing what, new things are occurring in real work as a result of leadership having been exercised. Innovation is now taking hold in some tangible way. This aspect of leadership necessarily includes observing how things are going with whatever is new or changed. Think of it as error detection, or noticing good results. The commitments to the people, the organization, and the truth provide the motivation.

For example, employees would begin saying new things to customers, or making new decisions when customers indicated they were not happy.

Adapting

Adapting may or may not occur based on what is observed in monitoring. If needed, the leadership move is to help create change, even within work that is about change itself! Call it course-correction, responding, or innovating as part of getting the work done in the best way possible. The commitments to the organization and the truth help here.

For example, changes would be made to expand or extend what is working well now with customers, and to jettison what did not work as expected.

Achieving

Achieving is getting it done, completing the job. The leadership role is to see that everything gets across the finish line, and to return to monitoring and adapting if that is threatened. A commitment to people, the organization, and the truth will fuel the hard work needed for the achievement to occur.

For example, the achievement would be happy customers.

Celebrating

Celebrating is recognizing, rewarding, commemorating, and creating emotion about what has drawn to a close. It is often overlooked in the rush of day-today work, however. This is a hazard, as failing to recognize the progress deflates motivation for future work. Celebrating reflects a commitment to people.

Celebrating may take the form of giving those involved some reward that could be significant, nominal, or just symbolic. Leadership that does this renews and even increases motivation.

Seeing anew

Seeing anew then renews the cycle. How do things look now? What is happening? These questions restart the cycle. In the example, it may be noticing that happy customers tend to bring in new customers through word of mouth, then imagining how that could be increased, and so on as the cycle restarts.

This model of leadership is just one way to look at how leadership can be exercised. Different cultures and workplaces will emphasize some aspects more than others. Sometimes only one or a few steps in the model will be the focus. However, the commitment to leadership means looking for, and then acting on, those places in an organization where a leader sees potential for improvement or problem-solving. This is truly walking the talk of leadership, engaging in what needs to be done for the organization to function at its best.

■■■■■ **PRACTICE TOOL**
Leading

As a leader, review what is happening in the organization that you are a part of, along the following dimensions. Be specific about your actions. An example is provided.

Leadership Action	Topic	Commitment
Seeing	I am noticing internal, unproductive conflict. I check for my own role in it.	Self, people, organization, truth
Imagining	I envision more collaborative work and better relationships.	Self, people, organization
Aligning	I begin talking with others about their perceptions, involving them in a shared desire to improve handling of conflict.	People, truth, leadership
Working	With coworkers, we look at what is happening, using a model for understanding and managing conflict. We apply that tool in a team exercise and learn about sources of our differences.	People, organization, truth
Adapting	We observe some good results and begin sharing the approach with other departments.	Organization, truth
Achieving	We achieve a significant reduction in unproductive conflict. Life is not perfect, but much better, and we use lapses as an opportunity to revisit the principles.	People, organization, truth
Celebrating	We order in pizza and cake, and in an appreciative exercise each recognize what others have done to make progress.	People
Seeing anew	We notice going forward how we manage conflict.	Self, people, organization, truth

■■■ Developing as a Leader

Now that we understand this cycle of thinking and action that constitutes a way of looking at how commitment to leadership shows up, let's turn our attention to how you can get *better* at that. The development of your leadership effectiveness is a key part of the commitment. How can you do that?

- Set goals
- Get feedback
- Get a coach or mentor
- Use assessments
- Take on developmental assignments
- Participate in a learning group
- Shadow others
- Participate in leadership development programs
- Read and journal
- Teach others

Set goals

It is fine to have a general intention to lead, but what does this mean to you? Where do you want to exercise leadership? To what ends? How will you know if you have succeeded?

These goals have to come out of your own sense of what the organization and people need, and where you can position yourself to help make that happen. For some, it may be in advocating a new course of action; for others, it could be helping a team in disarray to rebuild. The practice of noticing will help you clarify what is most important to you, so that you can engage others there and create leadership around those goals.

It is also important to periodically assess your goals and your progress toward them.

Get feedback

One of the most simple and powerful error-detection and correction channels is the least-used in organizations. Feedback from trusted and well-intentioned others gives you immediate information you can use to affirm or change course. Clearly, not every perception held by others will be shared by you, but the information can be taken as a valuable input to your thinking.

Asking for feedback means simply making a request along the lines of: "Can I get your feedback on how I handled that situation?" It's that simple. Some will be better at giving the information than others, but listen for what seems true to you. It's better to know.

Get a coach or mentor

Feedback can be particularly helpful coming from a coach or mentor, and he or she can offer many other kinds of information, as well. A mentor generally gives expert advice, based on experience and fine understanding of the organization or others. A coach does less of this, and more questioning to help you clarify your own thinking and actions. Of course, there is some overlap, but both can help you process events and think about lessons learned. The Action-Reflection Loop is a great tool a mentor or coach can use with you.

Use assessments

Assessments come in many forms—360s, type, conflict management skills, and so on. Some are self-report and others capture the perceptions of others. Leaders often report new insights into the self as a result of such assessments, and your goals should determine which assessments you take. Always, the question is what you do with the results—whether you make changes you feel are important, or whether the results fall on the floor.

Take on developmental assignments

In leadership development programs, developmental or stretch assignments invariably emerge as one of the most valuable learning and growth experiences participants have had. The reason is simple: Such work forces them out of their comfort zones into new and different environments, with personalities, culture, practices, and ways of working that question or challenge each leader's story. The adaptation, innovation, and flexing required to navigate through such situations is almost always recorded as a growth experience. It also broadens a leader's frame of reference as he or she sees across a wider swath of the organization. This improves knowledge of system-wide context and, therefore, decision-making.

Participate in a learning group

Another practice embedded in many leadership development programs is the creation and active use of a small group of people to whom an aspiring leader can go with questions, problems, and challenges. Such groups can be invaluable in helping a leader to frame or reframe what's at hand, think through solutions or options, and then operate. The trust and deep communication built in such small groups often allow leaders to disclose what may be hard otherwise. In deepening the conversation, new possibilities can emerge. Whether you are in a formal leadership development program or not, you can assemble your own group and help others as a member in the process.

This can take the form of a community of practice, knowledge-sharing, or skill development group. Toastmasters is an example of the last.

It's even more beneficial if this group includes a variety of skill sets and perspectives. For example, you may benefit by having people with expertise in strategic thinking, financial management, organizational savvy, execution and implementation, and emotional intelligence.

Shadow others

Observing other leaders at work is akin to a developmental assignment, but it's more observation than action. The success of this practice rests on the effectiveness of the person being shadowed, although it could be argued that much can be learned from observing ineffective leaders. (The danger is that the wrong behaviors may rub off.) Shadowing is best if you have an opportunity to discuss what you have seen with the person being shadowed.

Participate in leadership development programs

Some of the elements above are included in formal leadership development programs. Ranging from a few days to more than one year, such programs aim to equip participants with the skills they need to lead. Coursework, reading, assessments, simulations, and feedback are usually included. The key is to enter a program that is high-quality and relevant to your leadership goals.

Read and journal

Part of lifelong learning is staying invested in reading about leadership, and recording thoughts on your own journey. Sometimes, much can be accomplished, but you are not fully aware because it happens fast. Journaling can force you to stop and more clearly take notice of what is happening and what it means. Furthermore, reading back through your own journals will help you realize how far you have come.

Teach others

Educators know the highest retention rate of material comes when you are in a position to teach that material to others. You can think of leadership as sharing what you are learning. In addition, teaching it means you have to do it. This is walking the talk.

■■■■■ **PRACTICE TOOL**
Your Leadership Development

There are many ways to develop as a leader. Using the chart below, consider what you have done, what you are thinking about doing, and what you are willing to commit to in order to develop further as a leader. An example is provided in each case:

Practice	Sample Commitment	Commitment	Commitment	Commitment
Set goals	Write two goals related to leadership.			
Get feedback	Ask my colleagues for their feedback on my leadership.			
Get a coach or mentor	Contract with a coach for 3 months to explore both strengths and weaknesses.			
Use assessments	Take an emotional intelligence and leadership effectiveness assessment.			
Take on developmental assignments	Seek an assignment in a different division.			
Participate in a learning group	Join Toastmasters or other group devoted to learning and development.			
Shadow others	Observe how my colleagues in other departments run their meetings.			
Participate in a leadership development program	Find out from H.R. what opportunities there are.			
Read and journal	Commit to reading 10 books in the next year and note key thoughts that seem valuable to me.			
Teach others	Organize a session to discuss key messages learned about leadership.			

What Gets in the Way?

Understanding the promise of leadership and the ways in which it can be developed, the question becomes: What gets in the way?

Stated simply, by most accounts there is ample opportunity for the quality and effectiveness of leadership to improve. The U.S. Office of Personnel Management, in its 2006 study of nearly 221,000 federal government employees, found that less than 40 percent said their leaders generate high levels of motivation and commitment in the workforce.[1]

Similarly, in 2002 Gallup found that just over half of surveyed U.S. employees agree with the statement that the people who run companies are honest and ethical. Employees also said that only 66 percent of company leaders are trying to do what is best for their customers. Even fewer—only 44 percent—believed that the people who run most companies are trying to do what is best for their employees.[2]

Consequently, it is important to explore why this is so, as a means for you to do a self-check on any potential barriers you may experience. These chiefly include complacency, fear, and power.

Complacency

Complacency is not very complicated to understand. It simply means not caring enough to step up to effective leadership. To the complacent individual, the work and potential change involved are just not worth it. For many, it is something of a rut, and it cannot be equated with leadership.

Fear

In the brave new world of challenges and high stakes, it's not difficult to understand the need for the leader to take risks. It's another thing when you are the leader. The need to take risks can lead to fear.

Stated bluntly: There is no leadership without risk. It's that simple. This is not to say that risk should not be measured and managed carefully. But the idea of risk-free leadership is a contradiction in terms. The fearful leader is often characterized by an inability to make decisions.

The problem is that risk aversion may be part of the leader's story. Many people, over time, get promoted as they avoid any steps that might look like a mistake. This is a bureaucratic mindset that is inconsistent with leadership. The big bets that have to be placed around strategy, in particular, mean defining a course that may or may not work. There are no guarantees.

On a more everyday level, think of risk in communication. At what points are you stepping up to say what needs to be said, versus holding back? Are the truly important issues being surfaced, or buried? What are you risking in the conversations?

Again, how much risk any aspiring leader wants to hold is a personal calculation. Some fear any risk so much they never step up.

Power

Unfortunately, some leaders who acquire power formally or informally use it in a way that ultimately compromises their leadership effectiveness. Leaders who fall back on their position or authority to make things happen have very little social capital in the bank when they need support and cooperation from the workforce. As noted, reluctant compliance is a far cry from genuine commitment.

The ultimately humbling aspect of leadership is reflected in Franklin D. Roosevelt's observation: "It's a terrible thing to look over your shoulder when you are trying to lead and find no one there." Today, followers effectively vote with their feet on their leaders' effectiveness; hence the phrase that resonates among leaders: Talent walks. This is a powerless place to be. One participant in a leadership development workshop shared with me that his manager had threatened him, saying, "I control what goes on around here." He replied, "You don't control anything," and walked out of the job, starting his own successful business.

The question is: What caliber workforce is left behind under the outdated style of leadership?

I recently coached a leader on his fairly spectacular 360-degree assessment results. His employees rated him near the top of the scale on many aspects of leadership. In response to a question, he said, "Look, I'm responsible for what the department does, but I'm no different, and no better than any of the people I work with. I consider myself their equal. We have different responsibilities, but I think of us as equals."

Most of us have had the opportunity to glimpse the potential for leadership of free-thinking, accountable, and responsible people whose needs and aspirations are understood and respected. This kind of leadership can achieve so much more than "Because I give you a paycheck. That's why."

A commitment to leadership begins with a felt sense of the need to step up, to help an organization do its best work through some form of leading. Leaders can begin with clear seeing of what is happening within the organization, and from there move through a series of steps to make the leadership real and effective.

At the same time, they can work on their own development, learning more and more about their leadership. The practices presented in this chapter will help anyone hoping to increase leadership effectiveness.

Today, with all the challenges most organizations face, it can be tempting to sit back and refuse the call to lead. It's hard work, takes time, and creates risks, and there are no guarantees. However, choosing to embrace the leadership potential that is resident in all of us may prove transformational—for you, others, and the organization.

You won't know until you've tried.

Are you committed to leadership?

ENDNOTES

1. The U.S. Office of Personnel Management, http://www.fhcs2006.opm. gov/Reports/ResponseWPCT.asp?AGY=ALL&SECT=4 (accessed April 12, 2008).

2. The Gallup Organization, *The Gallup Management Journal,* http:// gmj.gallup.com/content/829/Gallup-Study-Finds-Many-Employees-Doubt-Ethics-Corporate-Leaders.aspx (accessed April 12, 2008).

RECOMMENDED READING

Goldsmith, Marshall. *What Got You Here Won't Get You There.* New York: Hyperion, 2007.

Maxwell, John. *The 21 Irrefutable Laws of Leadership.* Nashville, TN: Thomas Nelson, 1998.

CHAPTER 6 Final Thoughts

It is your choice now to reflect on the commitments, to find the place they hold and where they create energy and excitement in your own life, and to decide what you want to do as you move forward.

That choice begins with a commitment to your self—ultimately the key instrument of leadership, the ground out of which everything else happens. This is not code for selfishness, but self-awareness.

From there your choice moves to include others in the form of a commitment to people. While we all lead our own lives, real leadership begins to take hold when others are involved. Understanding their needs and potential helps you lead them effectively.

Your choice then occurs in the context of an organization, where people come together to accomplish something they care about collectively. Clarity on what matters most and how the organization is performing is part of the commitment.

Throughout the entire process, a commitment to the truth anchors everything in reality. This commitment is a disciplining, organizing, and guiding function. It is essential for leaders to be truth-tellers.

Your path culminates in a commitment to leadership. Incorporating the previous four commitments, leaders engage in a series of steps to notice what is occurring, and from there step out to begin the process of making life better. As they do so, they simultaneously, and intentionally, work on their own development, in many forms. Your chosen path can always be better.

The five commitments of leadership are a way to think about what you want to accomplish. They are not a strict equation, an easy five-step process, or a guarantee of success. Instead, they represent guideposts, helpful concepts for you to continually reference.

The journey never ends. No matter what you've done or not done in a leadership capacity, the very next conversation you have or action you take represents an opportunity to begin moving in the direction you believe is right. As George Eliot said, "It is never too late to become what you might have been."

It is my hope that continued reflection on the commitments, and practice of what they entail, can serve as a useful framework for you on this journey.

Good luck. Lead well.

APPENDIX

Empirical Research into Leadership

Clearly, leadership means many different things to many people. There are countless models, theories, and ideas. Depending on what you have experienced, a pithy quote or great story might seem to powerfully capture what leadership is all about, to you, at that moment.

At the same time, it is important to look at the topic from the perspective of exploring what really works, sustainably and over an extended time. The intention is to broaden any of our individual frames and grasp what, over the long haul, and across many different situations, seems to matter most. Here, we turn to data and empirical research.

Of all the contemporary research efforts in leadership, few if any can match the rigor and power of statistical findings presented in the following works:

- *The Extraordinary Leader,* by John Zenger and Joseph Folkman
- *Good to Great,* by Jim Collins
- *Working with Emotional Intelligence,* by Daniel Goleman
- *The Leadership Challenge,* by James Kouzes and Barry Posner.

This appendix summarizes how these individuals conducted their research, what they concluded, and finally, how those conclusions relate to the five commitments.

The Extraordinary Leader[1]

Joseph Folkman and John Zenger start out in *The Extraordinary Leader* with a simple question: What differentiates the best- and worst-performing leaders, as judged by the results of 360-degree assessments? They studied more than 200,000 such assessments on 20,000 leaders. They conclude with a metaphor of a tent, with the long pole in the middle representing character. The other keys to leadership effectiveness, as revealed by their research, are interpersonal skills, focus on results, personal capability, and leading organizational change.

While it is obvious that all these attributes relate to leadership, when we break the list down a bit we see that character comes from commitments to the self and the truth. Interpersonal skills are part of making commitments to the people and the self. A focus on results represents commitments to the organization and the people. Personal capability also reflects commitments to the truth and the self. A focus on leading change is part of commitments to the organization, people, and leadership.

▨▨▨ **Good to Great**[2]

Jim Collins takes a completely different approach in *Good to Great.* Rather than relying on internal perceptions of leadership effectiveness, he takes the analysis outside. He and his small army of researchers spent 15,000 hours carefully evaluating Fortune 500 companies that had posted significantly better-than-peer results over a sustained period. They simply looked for who had been doing the best, the longest.

Collins took a deliberately agnostic view of everything, holding no theories or ideas about what differentiated these companies. Instead, he backed up from the outstanding results to find out what was going on inside the "black box" that accounted for the results.

His first finding is that these companies had what he calls Level 5 leadership in all cases. A Level 5 leader moves beyond individual effectiveness, beyond being a good team player, and beyond being a competent manager or even leader, into the rarified air of building enduring greatness through a paradoxical blend of personal humility and professional will.

The enduring greatness Collins writes about emanates from the organization rather than from the leader. This view connects to the personal humility he identifies next: the notion that the leader is not an ego-propelled, publicity-seeking figure. Collins' leaders stand in stark contrast to some leader personalities we see today. He even notes that Level 5 leadership is at odds with the personal ambition that drives many people into positions of leadership.

Collins' work makes it ultimately practical for any leader to ask himself or herself: Is this about me, or the organization? It's an easy question to ask, but for some leaders, probably difficult to answer.

Clearly, personal humility is about a commitment to the self, while the drive for organizational results reflects a commitment to the organization and leadership.

Emotional Intelligence[3]

Not too many years ago the very use of the word "emotional" was practically verboten in organizations. Today, emotional intelligence is increasingly seen as critical for a leader.

Daniel Goleman reviewed huge databases of performance in creating his model of emotional intelligence, which consists of self-awareness, self-regulation, motivation, empathy, and social skills.

What is most striking about Goleman's work is his contention, buttressed again and again by empirical data, that emotional intelligence is a far better predictor of success in performance, and particularly leadership, than technical competence. Further, Goleman's research consistently shows that emotional intelligence matters more and more the higher in leadership one rises.

Self-awareness corresponds with commitments to the self and the truth. Self-regulation relates to the self and the people. Motivation is about the self, while empathy and social skills relate to commitments to people and the self.

The Leadership Challenge[4]

Kouzes and Posner studied tens of thousands of leaders, using a proprietary instrument called the Leadership Practices Inventory, as well as interviews and observations. They identified five fundamental attributes of leadership: challenging the process, inspiring a shared vision, enabling others to act, modeling the way, and encouraging the heart.

Challenging the process means continually seeking new ways, not being content to rely on last year's best practices. Inspiring a shared vision refers to shared meaning and the alignment of vision. Enabling others to act is empowerment. Modeling the way is setting the example, or walking the talk. Encouraging the heart means bringing out the best in everyone, around things they care about.

Challenging the process and inspiring a shared vision come from a commitment to the organization, leadership, and in the case of vision, people too. Enabling others to act is all about a commitment to people. Modeling the way comes from commitments to the self, people, and leadership, while encouraging the heart reflects a commitment to people.

ENDNOTES

1. Joseph Folkman and John Zenger, *The Extraordinary Leader: Turning Good Managers into Great Leaders* (New York: McGraw-Hill, 2002).
2. Jim Collins, *Good to Great: Why Some Companies Make the Leap … and Others Don't* (New York: HarperBusiness, 2001).
3. Daniel Goleman, *Emotional Intelligence: Why It Can Matter More Than IQ* (New York: Bantam Books, 1995).
4. James Kouzes and Barry Posner, *The Leadership Challenge* (San Francisco: Jossey-Bass, 1995).

INDEX

CPSIA information can be obtained at www.ICGtesting.com
Printed in the USA
BVOW06s0954280813

329691BV00005B/12/P